Foundations

A Walk Through the Foundational Truths of the Christian Faith

By: Aaron Shaw

Contents

Introduction

Welcome to *Foundations*, a 14-lesson workbook focused on doctrinal discipleship! This guide is designed to supplement—not replace—the teaching you receive through your local church. It was born not only out of necessity but also from a deep desire to share my passion for doctrine, theology, and the essential truths of the Christian faith. My hope is that as you engage with this material, a similar passion will be ignited within you—one that inspires you to grow deeper in your understanding of God.

It's important to note that the research and information presented here are not exhaustive—nor are they intended to be. Instead, this workbook aims to stir within you a desire for personal study, reflection, and prayerful discovery of God's truth. As you work through these lessons, I encourage you to carefully examine the Scriptures and Church history, ensuring everything aligns with God's Word.

In crafting this resource, I have intentionally avoided taking positions on issues that are heavily debated within the Church, provided they do not pertain to salvation. Whether you are discovering your faith for the first time or have been a believer for many years, I trust you will find something new, thought-provoking, or even challenging within these pages.

My prayer for you is simple: that you would fall in love with the God of the Bible as deeply as I have. May this journey equip you to not only understand what you believe but also to have the knowledge to support and share your faith. I hope it inspires you to anchor your faith in solid, biblical truths rather than relying solely on emotional experiences. Above all, may this workbook be a blessing, strengthening your overall understanding of the Christian faith.

1. The Inspiration of Scripture

Key Terms

1. **Inspiration** - The process by which God, through the Holy Spirit, guided human authors to write His Word, ensuring its truth and divine authority without overriding their personalities or styles (2 Timothy 3:16).
2. **Revelation** - The act of God making Himself and His will known to humanity, primarily through Scripture, but also through creation, Jesus Christ, and other means (Hebrews 1:1-2).
3. **Illumination** - The work of the Holy Spirit in helping believers understand, interpret, and apply the truths of Scripture (John 16:13).
4. **Inerrancy** - The belief that the original manuscripts of Scripture are without error in everything they affirm, including matters of faith, history, and science (Psalm 12:6; Proverbs 30:5).
5. **Authority** - The concept that Scripture, as the Word of God, has the ultimate right to command belief and obedience (2 Peter 1:20-21).
6. **Canon** - The collection of books recognized as divinely inspired and authoritative Scripture, forming the Old and New Testaments of the Bible (Luke 24:44; 2 Timothy 3:15-17).

What is the Bible?

At its core, the Bible is a book—but it is unlike any other. It is the divine Word of God, given to His creation to reveal Himself and His plan for humanity. Unlike most books, which are written for a specific audience or purpose, the Bible transcends time, culture, and language. It is intended for all people—every nation, every language, and every generation.

This extraordinary work consists of sixty-six books, written by approximately 40 authors over a span of about 1,500 years. The authors came from various walks of life, including shepherds, kings, prophets, and apostles, yet their writings form a unified message. Remarkably, the Bible was not originally divided into chapters and verses; these were added centuries later to make study and reference more accessible.

The Bible is divided into two main parts: the Old Testament and the New Testament.

- **The Old Testament** consists of 39 books and includes the law, history, prophecy, and wisdom literature of ancient Israel. It tells the story of creation, humanity's fall into sin, God's covenant with His chosen people, and the promises of a coming Savior. Through its narratives, prophecies, and poetry, it emphasizes humanity's need for redemption and foreshadows the coming of Jesus Christ.
- **The New Testament** is made up of 27 books and focuses on the fulfillment of God's plan through Jesus Christ. It begins with the Gospels, which recount the life, ministry, death, and resurrection of Jesus. It then transitions to the book of Acts, which details the history and growth of the early Church. Following Acts are epistles—letters written by apostles like Paul, Peter, and John to guide and encourage believers. The New Testament concludes with the book of Revelation, a prophetic

vision that reveals God's ultimate victory over sin and His plan for a new heaven and new earth.

Together, the Old and New Testaments provide a cohesive narrative of God's love, humanity's redemption, and the promise of eternal life through faith in Jesus Christ. The Bible is not merely a historical or religious document; it is the living and active Word of God (Hebrews 4:12), guiding believers in every aspect of life and pointing all people to the hope found in Christ.

How Did We Get The Canon of Scripture?

When referring to the canon of Scripture, we are speaking of the collection of books that make up the Old and New Testaments. The term "canon" refers to a standard or rule and is used to describe the set of books recognized as divinely inspired and authoritative. This concept is not unique to Christianity, as other religious traditions also have sacred texts that they consider canonical. However, the Christian canon stands out because of its unique validation through historical evidence, fulfilled prophecy, and its role in the life and teachings of Jesus Christ.

The Old Testament Canon

The Old Testament canon, comprising the first 39 books of the Bible, was written between approximately 1500 BC and 400 BC, though scholars debate the exact dates. These books include the Law (Torah), the historical books, the writings of the prophets, and wisdom literature.

The primary validation for the Old Testament canon comes from Jesus Himself. It is estimated that over one-tenth of Jesus' recorded words in the New Testament are quotations from the Old Testament. His frequent references to these texts, coupled with their widespread acceptance during His time, provide strong evidence of their divine authority. Additionally, New Testament authors collectively reference the Old Testament around 275 times, further demonstrating its foundational role in the Christian faith.

One notable exception is the Book of Enoch, which is referenced in Jude 1:14-15 but is not included in the current canon. Despite this, the consistent usage and endorsement of the 39 books by Jesus and His followers affirm their place as the Word of God. This is why the Christian Church has adopted this canon as authoritative.

The New Testament Canon

The New Testament consists of 27 books written between approximately 35 AD and 95 AD by about eight authors. These authors were either disciples of Jesus, His close associates, or witnesses to His resurrection. Their writings reflect a deep commitment to the truth of the gospel, and many were willing to die for their faith and the message they proclaimed.

The earliest known list of New Testament writings is found in the Muratorian Canon (or Muratorian Fragment). Discovered by Italian historian Ludovico Muratori in the Ambrosian Library in northern Italy and published in 1740, this document dates back to around 180 AD. It includes 22 of the 27 books in the current New Testament canon, excluding Hebrews, James, 1 and 2 Peter, and 3 John.

The Development of the Canon

In 364 AD, the Council of Laodicea convened in what is now modern-day Turkey. The council's members issued 60 rulings, two of which were significant for the canon. The 59th ruling declared that only canonical books should be read in church, and the 60th ruling specified a canon. This list included the 39 books of the Old Testament, the Book of Baruch and its extended ending (the Epistle of Jeremiah), and 26 of the 27 New Testament books, excluding Revelation.

The first complete list of New Testament books as we know them today appeared in the Thirty-Ninth Festal Letter written in 367 AD by Athanasius, Bishop of Alexandria. This list was later confirmed by the

Council of Hippo in 393 AD and the Council of Carthage in 397 AD, both of which affirmed the 27 books of the New Testament as authoritative.

These councils used specific criteria to determine whether a book should be included in the canon:

1. **Apostolic Authorship**: The author had to be an apostle or closely associated with one.
2. **Wide Acceptance**: The book needed to be widely accepted and used by the early church.
3. **Doctrinal Consistency**: The content had to align with established Christian teachings.
4. **Spiritual Integrity**: The book had to demonstrate high moral and spiritual values, reflecting divine inspiration.

The process of canonization demonstrates God's providence in preserving His Word. The Church did not create the canon; rather, it recognized and affirmed the texts inspired by the Holy Spirit. The canon of Scripture, as it exists today, reflects the unified message of God's redemptive plan for humanity through Jesus Christ and serves as a trustworthy guide for faith and life.

It is vital to acknowledge the sovereign hand of God in the canonization of both the Old and New Testaments. While human beings are inherently flawed—prone to mistakes, corruption, and ignorance—it is evident that God guided His Church in identifying and affirming His inspired Word. In essence, the Church did not determine the canon; God, in His sovereignty, ensured its recognition and preservation.

Why do we have so many different translations?

Jesus made it clear that we are to go into all the world and spread the message of the Good News. He said:
"Jesus came and told his disciples, 'I have been given all authority in heaven and on earth. Therefore, go and make disciples of all the nations, baptizing them in the name of the Father and the Son and the

Holy Spirit. Teach these new disciples to obey all the commands I have given you. And be sure of this: I am with you always, even to the end of the age.'" Matthew 28:18-20 NLT

This command requires that the message be communicated in a way that is easy for people from every nation to understand. As a result, there is a global effort to translate the Bible into every language. According to the Wycliffe Global Alliance's 2024 Global Scripture Access report, there are approximately 7,396 languages spoken worldwide. As of 2024, the distribution of Bible translations is as follows:

- **Complete Bible translations**: 756 languages
- **New Testament translations**: 1,726 languages
- **Some Bible portions translated**: 1,274 languages

This means that about 10% of the world's languages have a complete Bible, 23% have the New Testament, and 17% have some portions of the Bible translated. Additionally, many of these languages have multiple translations. For example, there are over 100 translations of the Bible in English alone.

The Bibles we read today are based on thousands of ancient manuscripts written in Hebrew and Greek. Every translation aims to balance two goals: staying faithful to the original language and ensuring readability in modern English. Translations are often categorized based on how closely they adhere to these goals: *Formal Equivalence* (Word-for-Word) and *Dynamic Equivalence* (Thought-for-Thought).

- **Formal Equivalence**: This translation philosophy seeks to match each Hebrew, Aramaic, and Greek word with its closest English equivalent while following proper English grammar. Examples include the *NASB, ESV,* and *KJV.*
- **Dynamic Equivalence**: This approach focuses on conveying the meaning or thought behind the original text, rather than translating word-for-word. Examples include the *NIV* and *NLT.*

It's also important to note that there is a third variation, which is not technically a translation but a paraphrase. Examples include *The Message* and *The Passion Translation*. These versions take more liberty with the text, aiming to make it more accessible but not strictly adhering to the original wording.

What do we mean when we say the Bible is inspired?

As Christians, we believe that the Bible is the Word of God, given to us through the inspiration of the Holy Spirit. While human authors wrote the text, it was God who guided the words. Evidence of this can be seen in the fulfillment of prophecy—over 300 prophecies specifically about Jesus. Additionally, the unity of scripture supports this claim. The Bible was written by around 40 different authors over a period of approximately 1,600 years. Despite the vast span of time and diverse authors, it contains no contradictions, and its themes remain consistent throughout. This unity could only have been achieved under the guidance of the Holy Spirit.

The Apostle Paul wrote this to Timothy:
"All Scripture is inspired by God and is useful to teach us what is true and to make us realize what is wrong in our lives. It corrects us when we are wrong and teaches us to do what is right. God uses it to prepare and equip His people to do every good work." 2 Timothy 3:16-17 NLT

The Apostle Peter wrote to believers in Asia Minor:
"Because of that experience, we have even greater confidence in the message proclaimed by the prophets. You must pay close attention to what they wrote, for their words are like a lamp shining in a dark place—until the Day dawns, and Christ the Morning Star shines in your hearts. Above all, you must realize that no prophecy in Scripture ever came from the prophet's own understanding, or from human initiative. No, those prophets were moved by the Holy Spirit, and they spoke from God." 2 Peter 1:19-21 NLT

When we say the Bible is inspired, we mean that it was written by human hands under the direction of the Holy Spirit. God was the source and origin of what was recorded. What we read today is the literal Word of the living God, the Creator of all life.

What did Jesus say about the Scripture?

Jesus emphasized the importance of knowing and understanding God's Word. In fact, when He was tempted in the desert, He responded with a powerful reminder of its value:
"But Jesus told him, 'No! The Scriptures say, "People do not live by bread alone, but by every word that comes from the mouth of God."""
Matthew 4:4 NLT. This quote is taken from Deuteronomy 8:3, and it not only underscores the significance of knowing God's Word, but also highlights the high regard Jesus placed on it. If Jesus, the Son of God, valued Scripture so deeply, how much more should we prioritize it in our own lives?

Jesus also said in Matthew 5:18, *"Not even the smallest detail of God's law will disappear until its purpose is achieved."* Matthew 5:18 NLT. In this statement, He affirms the lasting relevance and authority of what we call the "Books of the Law" in the Old Testament. Furthermore, in the Gospel of John, Jesus is quoted saying, *"Scriptures cannot be altered."* John 10:35 NLT. This statement reinforces the unchanging authority of God's Word.

Beyond these passages, it's remarkable to note that over one-tenth of Jesus' words recorded in the New Testament are drawn from the Old Testament. In fact, it has been estimated that 180 of the 1,800 verses in the Gospels that recount His teachings and conversations are either direct quotes or references to the Old Testament Scriptures. This is a significant amount of His teaching rooted in the Old Testament.

This should be deeply encouraging for us. It shows that not only did Jesus know the Scriptures intimately, but He also trusted in their truth and relied on them in His ministry. He understood them as the very Word of God, and He used them to teach, rebuke, and guide others. As His followers, we are called to do the same.

What did the Apostles say about Scripture?

The authors of the New Testament viewed their writings as Scripture and often referred to each other's works in this way. This suggests that they believed they had been granted divine authority by Jesus through the Holy Spirit to write with His guidance. Let's look at a few key examples to illustrate this.

The Apostle Paul, for instance, wrote the following:
"For the Scripture says, 'You must not muzzle an ox to keep it from eating as it treads out the grain.' And in another place, 'Those who work deserve their pay!'" 1 Timothy 5:18 NLT.
The second quote, *"Those who work deserve their pay!"* is not found in the Old Testament. The Greek phrase Paul uses matches exactly the phrase found in the Gospel of Luke: *"Those who work deserve their pay!"* Luke 10:7 NLT. This suggests that Paul considered Luke's Gospel, which includes the words of Jesus, to be Scripture. Furthermore, Paul places this writing on the same level of authority as the Old Testament, as he quotes both in the same sentence, further affirming their equal status.

We see similar examples when we look at what Peter had to say about Paul's writings:

"And remember, our Lord's patience gives people time to be saved. This is what our beloved brother Paul also wrote to you with the wisdom God gave him—speaking of these things in all of his letters. Some of his comments are hard to understand, and those who are ignorant and unstable have twisted his letters to mean something quite different, just as they do with other parts of Scripture. And this will result in their destruction." 2 Peter 3:15-16 NLT.
Notice the phrase, *"just as they do with other parts of Scripture."* Peter

clearly places Paul's letters in the same category as the Old Testament Scriptures, acknowledging their divine authority.

This is significant because earlier in the same letter, Peter wrote: *"I want you to remember what the holy prophets said long ago and what our Lord and Savior commanded through your apostles."* 2 Peter 3:2 NLT. Here, Peter is reminding the readers that God's commands come through the apostles. Since Peter himself was an apostle, he is implying that the Lord gives His commands through him as well, further reinforcing the authority of apostolic writings as Scripture.

These examples highlight that the authors of the New Testament, including Paul and Peter, viewed their own writings and the writings of others in the early Church as divinely inspired Scripture, placing them on the same level as the Old Testament texts. This recognition of the authority of their writings was foundational to the development of the New Testament canon.

Let's check out a few other examples.

"If you claim to be a prophet or think you are spiritual, you should recognize that what I am saying is a command from the Lord himself. But if you do not recognize this, you yourself will not be recognized."
1 Corinthians 14:37-38 NLT

"Therefore, we never stop thanking God that when you received his message from us, you didn't think of our words as mere human ideas. You accepted what we said as the very word of God—which, of course, it is. And this word continues to work in you who believe."
1 Thessalonians 2:13 NLT

"God blesses the one who reads the words of this prophecy to the church, and he blesses all who listen to its message and obey what it says, for the time is near."
Revelation 1:3 NLT

"But we belong to God, and those who know God listen to us. If they do not belong to God, they do not listen to us. That is how we know if someone has the Spirit of truth or the spirit of deception."
1 John 4:6 NLT

Why Does It Matter?

The Bible is far more than a collection of ancient writings; it is the revealed Word of God, offering direction, wisdom, and hope for our lives. As we navigate life's challenges and triumphs, Scripture provides timeless guidance on how to live in a way that contrasts with the world's values and standards. It not only recounts our history but also reveals the depth of humanity's fall into sin, our desperate need for salvation, and God's unwavering desire to redeem us. Above all, the Bible points us to the ultimate hope we have in Jesus Christ, the fulfillment of God's plan for salvation.

If Scripture is not divinely inspired, it ceases to be God's Word, and its authority is undermined. Without divine inspiration, the accounts recorded in the Bible could not be trusted as truth, nor could its guidance be relied upon for living a righteous life. If the Bible were merely a human creation, one of the foundational pillars of the Christian faith would collapse, leaving us without hope or purpose. The divine inspiration of Scripture is what distinguishes it as the ultimate source of truth, above human wisdom or tradition.

The doctrine of the inspiration of Scripture is essential to the Christian faith because it guarantees that what we read in the Bible is not merely human opinion or myth but the truth revealed by God Himself. It assures us that the teachings, historical accounts, and promises contained within its pages are trustworthy and authoritative. Without this foundation, our faith would lack substance, and our confidence in God's promises would be baseless.

The Bible's divine origin not only makes it unique but also reveals God's character—His holiness, love, justice, and mercy. Through its pages, we encounter a God who desires to be known and who provides a clear path for humanity's redemption. For Christians, Scripture is more than a historical record; it is the living and active Word of God (Hebrews 4:12), capable of transforming hearts, renewing minds, and equipping us for every good work (2 Timothy 3:16-17).

Further Study

1. What does the term "inspiration" mean in relation to the Bible, and how does it differentiate Scripture from other religious or philosophical texts?
2. How does the concept of divine inspiration explain the harmony and unity found throughout the Bible despite being written by multiple human authors over a span of centuries?
3. In 2 Timothy 3:16-17, Paul says that all Scripture is "inspired by God." What are the implications of this statement for how we view the authority of Scripture in our lives today?
4. How do fulfilled prophecies, such as those about Jesus, serve as evidence of the Bible's divine inspiration? Provide examples of specific prophecies that support this claim.
5. What role does the Holy Spirit play in the inspiration of Scripture, and how does this help explain the Bible's divine and human elements?
6. Why is the belief in the inspiration of Scripture essential to the Christian faith? What would be the consequences for our faith and understanding of God if Scripture were not inspired?

Bible project App

Bible Hub -
got questions.org -
Step bible App -
Amp -

Additional Notes:

2. Monotheism (The Unity of God)

Key Terms

1. **Monotheism** - The belief in the existence of one, and only one, God who is the Creator and Sustainer of all things. This is foundational to Christianity, Judaism, and Islam (Deuteronomy 6:4; Isaiah 45:5).
2. **Unity of God** - The concept that God is one in essence and being, indivisible in His nature, attributes, and will, as affirmed in Deuteronomy 6:4: "Hear, O Israel: The Lord our God, the Lord is one."
3. **Trinity** - The Christian doctrine that God exists as one essence in three distinct Persons—Father, Son, and Holy Spirit—who are coequal and coeternal, maintaining monotheism while emphasizing relational unity (Matthew 28:19; John 10:30).
4. **Sovereignty** - The attribute of God that highlights His ultimate authority and control over all creation, demonstrating His unique position as the one true God (Psalm 115:3; Isaiah 46:9-10).
5. **Omnipotence** - The quality of God being all-powerful, capable of accomplishing His will without limitation, affirming His singular supremacy over all things (Jeremiah 32:17; Revelation 19:6).
6. **Idolatry** - The worship of false gods, idols, or anything other than the one true God, which is strictly prohibited in monotheistic faiths (Exodus 20:3-5; Isaiah 44:6-20).

What is Monotheism?

Monotheism is the belief in the existence of only one God, who is supreme and sovereign over all creation. While this belief has been practiced for thousands of years, the term "monotheism" itself is relatively new, first appearing in English in 1660, attributed to philosopher Henry More. Monotheism is central to several major world religions, including Christianity, Islam, and

Judaism is widely regarded as the oldest monotheistic religion, originating with God's covenant with Abraham, as described in the book of Genesis. This faith introduced the concept of a single, all-powerful, and personal God who created and sustains the universe. The Shema, found in Deuteronomy 6:4—*"Hear, O Israel: The Lord our God, the Lord is one"*—is a foundational declaration of Jewish monotheism. Judaism laid the groundwork for both Christianity and Islam, emphasizing the worship of one God and the moral and ethical standards He commands.

Christianity emerged from the roots of Judaism, fulfilling its prophecies through the life, death, and resurrection of Jesus Christ. Christians affirm monotheism while also embracing the doctrine of the Trinity—the belief that the one God exists in three distinct persons: Father, Son, and Holy Spirit. This doctrine distinguishes Christianity from other monotheistic religions and highlights its unique understanding of God's relational nature. The teachings of Jesus and the apostles in the New Testament reinforce the belief in one God (e.g., 1 Corinthians 8:6; Ephesians 4:6).

Islam, which arose in the 7th century AD, also claims monotheism as a central tenet. Muslims worship Allah, whom they regard as the same God worshiped by Jews and Christians. However, Islam is often considered a deviation from the established Abrahamic faiths of Judaism and Christianity. While Islam acknowledges figures like Abraham, Moses, and Jesus, it rejects key Christian doctrines such as the deity of Jesus and the concept of the Trinity. Instead, Islam views Muhammad as the final prophet and the Qur'an as the ultimate revelation of God.

What do we Believe?

As Christians, we believe in one supreme God, the Creator and Sustainer of all life and everything in existence. This God transcends time, having neither beginning nor end. He has always existed and will always exist, embodying infinite power, wisdom, and love.

We also believe that this one God exists as three distinct persons—God the Father, God the Son, and God the Holy Spirit—yet remains one God. This concept, known as the Trinity, is a core belief of Christianity. Though it is a profound mystery that cannot be fully understood by human reasoning, it is clearly revealed in Scripture. *(We will explore the Trinity in greater detail in the next chapter to gain a deeper understanding of its significance and its role in shaping our faith.)*

The prophet Isaiah had this to say concerning the unity of God:

"This is what the Lord says—Israel's King and Redeemer, the Lord of Heaven's Armies: 'I am the First and the Last; there is no other God.'" Isaiah 44:6 NLT

Isaiah's words reflect the foundational belief of the Jewish faith: there is only one God. This conviction formed the core of their belief system, a faith that stood in stark contrast to the polytheistic cultures surrounding them. In a world where pagan nations worshiped numerous gods representing various aspects of life and nature, the Jewish people proclaimed the supremacy and singularity of the one true God, the Creator and Sustainer of all things.

The Apostle Paul echoed this belief when addressing the church in Corinth, a city heavily influenced by paganism and idolatry:

"So, what about eating meat that has been offered to idols? Well, we all know that an idol is not really a god and that there is only one God. There may be so-called gods both in heaven and on earth, and some people actually worship many gods and many Lords. But for us, There is one God, the Father, by whom all things were created, and for whom we live. And there is one Lord, Jesus Christ, through whom all things were created, and through whom we live."
1 Corinthians 8:4-6 NLT

Paul's words affirm the unity of God while highlighting the Christian understanding of the relationship between God the Father and Jesus Christ. This perspective builds on the Jewish monotheistic tradition, emphasizing that all creation exists by and for God, with Jesus as the divine agent of creation and redemption. Together, these passages remind us of the unique identity and unity of God, central to both Jewish and Christian faiths.

Where did it begin?

The Bible begins like no other ancient text. It boldly claims that the heavens and the earth were created by a single, sovereign deity. This God operates without assistance, interference, or rival, exercising complete authority over creation. This uniqueness is striking: the Creator in Genesis has no pantheon, no conflicts over supremacy, and no unmet needs driving creation. Instead, the opening chapters of Genesis reveal a God who is entirely self-sufficient and all-powerful.

"In the beginning God created the heavens and the earth."
Genesis 1:1 NLT

"So the creation of the heavens and the earth and everything in them was completed. On the seventh day God had finished his work of creation, so he rested from all his work. And God blessed the seventh

day and declared it holy, because it was the day when he rested from
all his work of creation."
Genesis 2:1-3 NLT

Shortly after creation, things begin to go awry. Humanity fails to recognize the supremacy of God and turns away from Him in sin. This single act of disobedience—eating from the forbidden tree—sets in motion a cataclysmic chain of events. God's creation is marred by sin, and humanity is expelled from the Garden of Eden. As Genesis 4-11 unfolds, we see the consequences of humanity's rebellion: violence, corruption, and the eventual judgment of the flood. While the Bible provides limited details about this time, it is evident that God's creation drifted further from Him, largely forgetting their origins and purpose.

In Genesis 12, however, we see a dramatic turning point. God reveals Himself to Abram (later renamed Abraham in Genesis 17) and makes a covenant that will shape the course of history:

"The Lord had said to Abram, 'Leave your native country, your relatives, and your father's family, and go to the land that I will show you. I will make you into a great nation. I will bless you and make you famous, and you will be a blessing to others. I will bless those who bless you and curse those who treat you with contempt. All the families on earth will be blessed through you.'"
Genesis 12:1-3 NLT

At this time, humanity had largely turned to polytheism and idolatry, worshiping many gods and practicing pagan rituals. In contrast, Abraham and his descendants chose to worship the one true God, known to them by titles such as *Elohim* (a plural form meaning "God" or "Lord") and *El Shaddai* ("God Almighty"). This distinct monotheism set Abraham and his lineage apart from the surrounding cultures.

While the nature of Hebrew worship before the Exodus remains unclear, everything began to change when God revealed Himself to

Moses on Mount Sinai, introducing Himself as *Yahweh* (Exodus 3:14). This personal name marked a new phase in God's ongoing revelation to His people, highlighting His unity, faithfulness, and desire for a relationship with His creation. Through Moses, God gave the Law, which became a foundational aspect of Hebrew worship and identity, revealing His holiness and moral will.

This process of divine revelation continued throughout history. The Law laid the groundwork for the messages of the prophets, who called people back to faithfulness and revealed deeper aspects of God's character. Through Scripture, God's unity, power, and love were made known, allowing humanity to better understand what He is like and how He desires to relate to His creation.

The Bible, beginning with Genesis, reveals a God who is not distant or impersonal but deeply invested in His creation. Through His ongoing revelation, humanity has come to know there is one singular God who is sovereign, holy, and worthy of worship.

Why does it matter?

The oneness of God is foundational to the first and greatest commandment of both the Old and New Testaments. In Deuteronomy, Moses not only proclaims God's unity but also calls on Israel to acknowledge His singular worth:

"Listen, O Israel! The Lord is our God, the Lord alone. And you must love the Lord your God with all your heart, all your soul, and all your strength."
Deuteronomy 6:4-5 NLT

This passage is known as the Shema, one of the most famous prayers in the Bible and a daily prayer for the ancient Israelites. In this moment, Moses is addressing a new generation of Israel as they prepare to enter the Promised Land. He urges them not to repeat the mistakes of their parents' generation, who disobeyed God and faced the consequences. Moses emphasizes that for the people to experience the fullness of God's blessings, they must listen to and love God fully, above all else.

In the New Testament, Jesus affirms this commandment as the greatest when debating with teachers of religious law:

"Jesus replied, 'The most important commandment is this: "Listen, O Israel! The Lord our God is the one and only Lord. And you must love the Lord your God with all your heart, all your soul, all your mind, and all your strength."'
Mark 12:29-30 NLT

Since the fall of man, humanity has consistently placed creation in the position reserved for the Creator. We are inherently worshipful beings, designed to glorify God. Yet, in the absence of divine revelation, we often worship incorrectly, directing our devotion toward idols or worldly pursuits. This misplaced worship leads to spiritual and, ultimately, physical destruction. God created us to worship Him alone, and what or whom we worship profoundly matters. Recognizing and understanding the unity of God is critical to rightly orienting our lives.

Jesus spoke about this during the Sermon on the Mount:

"No one can serve two masters. For you will hate one and love the other; you will be devoted to one and despise the other. You cannot serve God and be enslaved to money."
Matthew 6:24 NLT

James, the half-brother of Jesus, also addressed divided loyalty:

"But when you ask him, be sure that your faith is in God alone. Do not waver, for a person with divided loyalty is as unsettled as a wave of the sea that is blown and tossed by the wind."
James 1:6 NLT

When we discover who God is, we are able to put Him in His proper place—above all else, as the supreme authority over our lives. When God is in His rightful place, we begin to understand our need for Him and His guidance. Recognition of the one true God is essential for our spiritual success and stability. It allows us to live as we were created to live: in worshipful obedience to the Creator, who alone is worthy of our devotion.

Who is God?

Thinking correctly about God is of utmost importance because having a false idea about God amounts to idolatry. A helpful summary definition of God is: *"the Supreme Being; the Creator and Ruler of all that exists; the Self-existent One who is perfect in power, goodness, and wisdom."* God is not one among many deities to choose from, nor can He be equated with other supposed gods. He alone is sovereign and supreme.

As the Creator, God made everything that exists, and He sustains all of creation. The Bible reveals that God the Father, by the power of God the Holy Spirit and through the agency of God the Son, Jesus Christ, brought the universe into being. This truth underscores the doctrine of the Trinity: that God is one being in three distinct persons— Father, Son, and Holy Spirit—perfectly unified in essence and purpose.

1. God Is Infinite – He is Self-Existing, Without Origin

"He existed before anything else, and he holds all creation together."
Colossians 1:17 NLT

2. God Is Immutable – He Never Changes

""I am the Lord, and I do not change. That is why you descendants of Jacob are not already destroyed."
Malachi 3:6 NLT

3.   God Is Self Sufficient - He Has No Needs

"The Father has life in himself, and he has granted that same life-giving power to his Son."
John 5:26 NLT

4.   God Is Omnipotent - He Is All Powerful

"The Lord merely spoke, and the heavens were created. He breathed the word, and all the stars were born."
Psalms 33:6 NLT
(See also Job 11:7-11)

5.   God Is Omniscient - He Is All Knowing

"Remember the things I have done in the past. For I alone am God! I am God, and there is none like me. Only I can tell you the future before it even happens. Everything I plan will come to pass, for I do whatever I wish."
Isaiah 46:9-10 NLT

6.   God Is Omnipresent - He Is Always Everywhere

"I can never escape from your Spirit! I can never get away from your presence! If I go up to heaven, you are there; if I go down to the grave, you are there. If I ride the wings of the morning, if I dwell by the farthest oceans, even there your hand will guide me, and your strength will support me."
Psalms 139:7-10 NLT

7. God Is Wise - He Is Full Of Perfect, Unchanging Wisdom

"Oh, how great are God's riches and wisdom and knowledge! How impossible it is for us to understand his decisions and his ways!"
Romans 11:33 NLT

8. God Is Faithful - He Is Infinitely, Unchangingly True

"If we are unfaithful, he remains faithful, for he cannot deny who he is."
2 Timothy 2:13 NLT

9. God Is Good – He Is Infinitely, Unchangingly Kind and Full of Good Will

"Taste and see that the Lord is good. Oh, the joys of those who take refuge in him!"
Psalms 34:8 NLT

10. God Is Just – He Is Infinitely, Unchangeably Right and Perfect in All He Does

"He is the Rock; his deeds are perfect. Everything he does is just and fair. He is a faithful God who does no wrong; how just and upright he is!"
Deuteronomy 32:4 NLT

11. God Is Merciful – He is Infinitely, Unchangeably Compassionate and Kind

"For God said to Moses, "I will show mercy to anyone I choose, and I will show compassion to anyone I choose." So it is God who decides to show mercy. We can neither choose it nor work for it."
Romans 9:15-16 NLT

12. God Is Gracious – God Is Infinitely Inclined to Spare the Guilty

"The Lord is merciful and compassionate, slow to get angry and filled with unfailing love."
Psalms 145:8 NLT

13. God Is L̶o̶v̶i̶n̶g̶ Love – God Infinitely, Unchangingly Loves Us

"Dear friends, let us continue to love one another, for love comes from God. Anyone who loves is a child of God and knows God. But anyone who does not love does not know God, for God is love."
1 John 4:7-8 NLT

14. God Is Holy – He is Infinitely, Unchangingly Perfect
"Holy, holy, holy is the Lord God, the Almighty— the one who always was, who is, and who is still to come.""
Revelation 4:8 NLT

15. God Is Glorious – He is Infinitely Beautiful and Great

"His coming is as brilliant as the sunrise. Rays of light flash from his hands, where his awesome power is hidden."
Habakkuk 3:4 NLT

Further Study

1. What is monotheism, and how does it differ from polytheism and atheism?
2. How does the Christian doctrine of the Trinity maintain the belief in one God while acknowledging the Father, Son, and Holy Spirit?
3. What biblical passages explicitly affirm the belief in one God, and how do these verses shape the foundation of Christian monotheism?
4. How does Christian monotheism influence the way believers understand God's sovereignty, authority, and relationship with His creation?
5. Why is the concept of one God essential to the gospel message and the Christian understanding of salvation?
6. What challenges does monotheism present to modern cultural and religious pluralism, and how can Christians respond to these challenges?

Additional Notes:

3. The Trinity

Key Terms

1. **Trinity** - The Christian doctrine that God is one being in three distinct Persons—Father, Son, and Holy Spirit—coequal, coeternal, and of the same essence, yet distinct in roles (Matthew 28:19; 2 Corinthians 13:14).

2. **Personhood** - The quality of each member of the Trinity as a distinct Person, having unique roles and relationships within the Godhead while sharing the same divine essence (John 14:26; John 10:30).

3. **Essence** - The single, indivisible nature of God that all three Persons of the Trinity share fully and equally, emphasizing God's unity (Deuteronomy 6:4; John 17:21).

4. **Coeternality** - The attribute of the Father, Son, and Holy Spirit existing eternally without beginning or end, affirming their equal and timeless divinity (John 1:1-2; Hebrews 9:14).

5. **Economic Trinity** - The way the three Persons of the Trinity relate to each other and fulfill distinct roles in creation, redemption, and sanctification (e.g., the Father sends, the Son redeems, the Spirit sanctifies) (Ephesians 1:3-14).

6. **Modalism** - A heretical view that denies the distinct Persons of the Trinity, claiming that God manifests Himself in different "modes" or forms at different times, rather than existing simultaneously as three Persons (refuted by passages like Matthew 3:16-17).

What is the trinity?

A.W. Tozer said, "The most important thing about you is what you think about when you think about God."

It's important to first realize that the Trinity and God are one in the same, so every characteristic that applies to God also applies to the Godhead. *(Please see the 15 attributes in the previous chapter for the characteristics of God)* We should also keep in mind that the word Trinity is not found in scripture anywhere, but as you will come to see in the following paragraphs, the concept certainly does. So, let's begin by looking at some basic truths.

- The Father is God.
- The Son is God.
- The Holy Spirit is God.
- The Father is not the Son or the Holy Spirit.
- The Son is not the Father or the Holy Spirit.
- The Holy Spirit is not the Father or the Son.
- There are not three gods.

Simply put, the Trinity refers to the Christian understanding of the Godhead as one God in three persons: Father, Son, and Holy Spirit. The doctrine of the Trinity belongs to *revealed theology*, not *natural theology*.

Natural theology is the study or understanding of God through human reason and observation of the natural world, unaided by special or supernatural revelation. It is sometimes referred to as rational theology.

Revealed theology, on the other hand, refers to knowledge of God that comes through divine revelation. This includes the Word of God (the Bible), messengers like angels, prophets, Jesus Christ, and the Holy

Spirit. The Trinity is a truth that is known only because God has chosen to reveal it through Scripture and special revelation.

The Trinity is best summarized in the Athanasian Creed, named after Athanasius, a fourth-century bishop of Alexandria and a prominent defender of Trinitarian doctrine. Before examining the creed, it is important to clarify a key term it uses: "Catholic." In this context, Athanasius is not referring to the Roman Catholic Church as we commonly think of it today. Instead, the term "Catholic" comes from the Greek word *katholikos*, a combination of *kata* (concerning) and *holos* (whole). According to the *Oxford Dictionary of English Etymology*, "Catholic" originally meant "universal" or "general." It was applied to all Christians, emphasizing the universal Church as the Body of Christ, encompassing all believers.

The Athanasian Creed is as follows.

Whoever wants to be saved should above all cling to the catholic faith. Whoever does not guard it whole and inviolable will doubtless perish eternally.
Now this is the catholic faith: We worship one God in trinity and the Trinity in unity, neither confusing the persons nor dividing the divine being.
For the Father is one person, the Son is another, and the Spirit is still another.
But the deity of the Father, Son, and Holy Spirit is one, equal in glory, coeternal in majesty.
What the Father is, the Son is, and so is the Holy Spirit.
Uncreated is the Father; uncreated is the Son; uncreated is the Spirit.
The Father is infinite; the Son is infinite; the Holy Spirit is infinite.
Eternal is the Father; eternal is the Son; eternal is the Spirit: And yet there are not three eternal beings, but one who is eternal; as there are not three uncreated and unlimited beings, but one who is uncreated and unlimited.
Almighty is the Father; almighty is the Son; almighty is the Spirit: And yet there are not three almighty beings, but one who is almighty.

Thus the Father is God; the Son is God; the Holy Spirit is God: And yet there are not three gods, but one God.

Thus the Father is Lord; the Son is Lord; the Holy Spirit is Lord: And yet there are not three lords, but one Lord.

As Christian truth compels us to acknowledge each distinct person as God and Lord, so catholic religion forbids us to say that there are three gods or lords.

The Father was neither made nor created nor begotten; the Son was neither made nor created, but was alone begotten of the Father; the Spirit was neither made nor created, but is proceeding from the Father and the Son.

Thus there is one Father, not three fathers; one Son, not three sons; one Holy Spirit, not three spirits.

And in this Trinity, no one is before or after, greater or less than the other; but all three persons are in themselves, coeternal and coequal; and so we must worship the Trinity in unity and the one God in three persons.

Whoever wants to be saved should think thus about the Trinity.

It is necessary for eternal salvation that one also faithfully believe that our Lord Jesus Christ became flesh.

For this is the true faith that we believe and confess: That our Lord Jesus Christ, God's Son, is both God and man.

He is God, begotten before all worlds from the being of the Father, and he is man, born in the world from the being of his mother — existing fully as God, and fully as man with a rational soul and a human body; equal to the Father in divinity, subordinate to the Father in humanity.

Although he is God and man, he is not divided, but is one Christ.

He is united because God has taken humanity into himself; he does not transform deity into humanity.

He is completely one in the unity of his person, without confusing his natures.

For as the rational soul and body are one person, so the one Christ is God and man.

He suffered death for our salvation. He descended into hell and rose again from the dead.

He ascended into heaven and is seated at the right hand of the Father.

He will come again to judge the living and the dead.
At his coming all people shall rise bodily to give an account of their
own deeds.
Those who have done good will enter eternal life, those who have done
evil will enter eternal fire.
This is the catholic faith.
One cannot be saved without believing this firmly and faithfully.

It is important to note that while the creed asserts belief in the Trinity as essential to salvation, I do not consider this to be entirely accurate. A belief or complete understanding of the Trinity, while significant, is not a requirement for salvation. Scripture clearly teaches that salvation comes through faith in Jesus Christ and His work on the cross. As Ephesians 2:8-9 states, we are saved by grace through faith, not by our own understanding or works.

Although belief in the Trinity is not necessary for salvation, it remains a vital truth of the Christian faith. The doctrine of the Trinity reveals important aspects of God's nature and helps us to better understand His work in creation, redemption, and our relationship with Him. While it is not the basis of salvation, it should not be dismissed as unimportant.

"If you openly declare that Jesus is Lord and believe in your heart that God raised him from the dead, you will be saved. For it is by believing in your heart that you are made right with God, and it is by openly declaring your faith that you are saved. As the Scriptures tell us, "Anyone who trusts in him will never be disgraced.""
Romans 10:9-11 NLT

What examples of the trinity do we see in scripture?

A popular myth today suggests that the doctrine of the Trinity was invented in the fourth century at the Council of Nicaea. This claim is false. From the earliest days of the Church, Christians were teaching the foundational truths of the Trinity as revealed in Scripture.

Around 318 AD, controversy arose over the teachings of Arius, a presbyter in Alexandria. Arius denied the full divinity of Jesus Christ, claiming that He was a created being rather than coeternal with God the Father. This heresy, later known as Arianism, spread quickly and created division within the Church. In response, it became crucial for Church leaders to affirm what had been an essential part of the faith from the beginning.

On June 19, 325 AD, over 300 bishops gathered at the First Ecumenical Council in Nicaea. This council produced the Nicene Creed, a statement of faith that affirmed the divinity of Jesus Christ and clarified the Church's understanding of the Trinity. The creed did not invent the doctrine of the Trinity but confirmed the truths already taught in Scripture and upheld by the early Church.

Evidence of the Trinity can be seen from the very beginning of Christianity. For instance, in the Great Commission, Jesus instructs His followers to baptize *"in the name of the Father and the Son and the Holy Spirit"* (Matthew 28:19). Similarly, the Apostle Paul highlights the Trinity in his benediction to the Corinthians:

"May the grace of the Lord Jesus Christ, the love of God, and the fellowship of the Holy Spirit be with you all."
2 Corinthians 13:14 NLT

These passages demonstrate that the concept of the Trinity was not a later invention but a foundational truth of the Christian faith, rooted in the teachings of Jesus and the apostles.

Let's take a moment to examine a few passages that reference each member of the Godhead as Deity. This list is not exhaustive, nor does it explore every aspect of the topic. I encourage you to dig deeper and study these Scriptures further on your own.

The Father as God

The Bible consistently refers to God the Father as Deity:

"May God our Father and the Lord Jesus Christ give you grace and peace."
Philippians 1:2 NLT

"I am writing to all of you in Rome who are loved by God and are called to be his own holy people. May God our Father and the Lord Jesus Christ give you grace and peace."
Romans 1:7 NLT

Jesus as God

The divinity of Jesus is also affirmed in Scripture:

"While we look forward with hope to that wonderful day when the glory of our great God and Savior, Jesus Christ, will be revealed."
Titus 2:13 NLT

"Abraham, Isaac, and Jacob are their ancestors, and Christ himself was an Israelite as far as his human nature is concerned. And he is God, the one who rules over everything and is worthy of eternal praise! Amen."
Romans 9:5 NLT

The Holy Spirit as God

The Bible also reveals the Holy Spirit as God:

"Then Peter said, 'Ananias, why have you let Satan fill your heart? You lied to the Holy Spirit, and you kept some of the money for yourself. The property was yours to sell or not sell, as you wished. And after selling it, the money was also yours to give away. How could you do a thing like this? You weren't lying to us but to God!'"
Acts 5:3-4 NLT

"Don't you realize that all of you together are the temple of God and that the Spirit of God lives in you?"
1 Corinthians 3:16 NLT

Three Distinct Persons

Not only is each member of the Trinity fully God, but they are also uniquely distinct persons. At the baptism of Jesus by John in the Jordan River, we get a unique view of all three persons present at one time:

"After his baptism, as Jesus came up out of the water, the heavens were opened and he saw the Spirit of God descending like a dove and settling on him. And a voice from heaven said, 'This is my dearly loved Son, who brings me great joy.'"
Matthew 3:16-17 NLT

In John's Gospel, Jesus clearly distinguishes between the Father, the Son, and the Holy Spirit while emphasizing their unity and cooperation. As He prepares His disciples for His departure, He points to the distinct roles of each person of the Trinity:

"But when the Father sends the Advocate as my representative—that is, the Holy Spirit—he will teach you everything and will remind you of everything I have told you."
John 14:26 NLT

We see this same distinction and unity in the book of Acts:

"Once when he was eating with them, he commanded them, 'Do not leave Jerusalem until the Father sends you the gift he promised, as I told you before. John baptized with water, but in just a few days you will be baptized with the Holy Spirit.'"
Acts 1:4-5 NLT

What roles do each member of the Godhead play?

While the members of the Trinity are co-equal and co-eternal, they fulfill distinct roles or functions within the Godhead. Some describe these distinctions as follows: the Father is the Creator, the Son is the

Redeemer, and the Holy Spirit is the Sanctifier, the one who sets believers apart. Another perspective identifies the Father as the source of all things, the Son as the agent (the one who acts on behalf of the Father), and the Holy Spirit as the means by which the Father works. These distinctions can help us understand the unique roles of each Person of the Trinity while maintaining their unity.

We can begin to see this "division of labor" in the following passages:

"May the grace of the Lord Jesus Christ, the love of God, and the fellowship of the Holy Spirit be with you all."
2 Corinthians 13:14 NLT

"God the Father knew you and chose you long ago, and his Spirit has made you holy. As a result, you have obeyed him and have been cleansed by the blood of Jesus Christ. May God give you more and more grace and peace."
1 Peter 1:2 NLT

It is important to note that while each member of the Trinity has distinct roles, they always work in full cooperation with one another. In every divine act, all three members are actively involved. For example:

- **Creation:** While the Father is preeminently the Creator, Scripture affirms that the Son and the Spirit were also involved in creation.
- **Redemption:** The Son is the Redeemer, sent by the Father and empowered by the Spirit to accomplish the work of salvation.
- **Sanctification:** The Spirit is the Sanctifier, the one who sets believers apart, but this work is carried out in unity with the Father and the Son.

The Bible consistently emphasizes this cooperation, demonstrating that each member of the Trinity is personally involved in all aspects of God's work. Although they fulfill different roles, the Father,

Son, and Holy Spirit operate in perfect unity, reflecting the harmony and oneness of the Godhead.

The members of the Trinity point to each other.

Though we cannot know for certain, I personally believe that when we stand in the presence of God, each person of the Trinity will be "pointing" to the other. This belief stems from the example we see in Scripture, where the members of the Trinity consistently glorify and testify about one another.

"And a voice from heaven said, 'This is my dearly loved Son, who brings me great joy.'"
Matthew 3:17 NLT

"So Jesus explained, 'I tell you the truth, the Son can do nothing by himself. He does only what he sees the Father doing. Whatever the Father does, the Son also does.'"
John 5:19 NLT

"But when the Father sends the Advocate as my representative—that is, the Holy Spirit—he will teach you everything and will remind you of everything I have told you.'"
John 14:26 NLT

"But I will send you the Advocate—the Spirit of truth. He will come to you from the Father and will testify all about me.'"
John 15:26 NLT

In these passages, we see how the Father glorifies the Son, the Son submits to and reflects the Father, and the Holy Spirit points back to both the Father and the Son. This mutual glorification and perfect unity are hallmarks of the Trinity's relationship.

One common mistake we often make in the Church today is placing undue focus on one person of the Trinity at the expense of the others. While it is natural to emphasize certain aspects of God's work—

such as the Father as Creator, the Son as Redeemer, or the Holy Spirit as Sanctifier—it is crucial to remember that each person of the Trinity is equally divine and inseparably one. The Unity of God means that the Father, Son, and Holy Spirit work together in perfect harmony, never acting independently or in isolation.

The Trinity is a profound mystery that cannot be fully explained by human reasoning, yet it reveals the unique nature of God as one being in three distinct persons: the Father, the Son, and the Holy Spirit, who are co-equal, co-eternal, and unified in essence and purpose. This doctrine demonstrates that God is relational and personal, existing in perfect harmony and mutual glorification. It provides a framework for understanding God's work in creation, redemption, and sanctification, with the Father as the source, the Son as the Redeemer, and the Spirit as the Sanctifier. As believers seek to grow in their knowledge of God, they must approach this mystery with humility and reverence, allowing the unity and love of the Trinity to inspire awe, worship, and a deeper relationship with Him.

Further Study

1. What does the doctrine of the Trinity teach about the nature of God, and why is it central to the Christian faith?
2. How do passages like Matthew 28:19 ("baptizing them in the name of the Father and the Son and the Holy Spirit") and 2 Corinthians 13:14 demonstrate the concept of the Trinity?
3. How does the relationship between the Father, Son, and Holy Spirit demonstrate both unity and distinction within the Godhead?
4. What are some common misunderstandings or heresies related to the Trinity, such as modalism or Arianism, and how does orthodox Christian doctrine address them?
5. How does the Trinity reveal the relational nature of God, and what implications does this have for our understanding of love and community?
6. Why is it important for Christians to worship God as Father, Son, and Holy Spirit, rather than focusing exclusively on one Person of the Trinity?

Additional Notes:

4. The Deity of Jesus

Key Terms

1. **Incarnation** - The Christian belief that Jesus, the eternal Son of God, took on human flesh and became fully God and fully man (John 1:14; Philippians 2:6-8).
2. **Immanuel** - A name for Jesus meaning "God with us," signifying His divine nature and presence with humanity, as prophesied in Isaiah 7:14 and fulfilled in Matthew 1:23.
3. **Logos** - A Greek term meaning "Word," used in John 1:1-14 to describe Jesus as the eternal Word of God, active in creation and fully divine.
4. **Preexistence**- The teaching that Jesus existed as God the Son before His incarnation, affirming His eternal divine nature (John 8:58; Colossians 1:17).
5. **Hypostatic Union** - The theological term describing the union of Jesus' divine and human natures in one Person, fully God and fully man without mixing or diminishing either nature (Colossians 2:9; Hebrews 4:15).
6. **Christology** - The field of theology that studies the person and work of Jesus Christ, including His deity, humanity, and role in salvation (Matthew 16:16; Hebrews 1:3).

"Jesus Christ was either a liar, a lunatic, or He was who He said He was" — C.S. Lewis

What Do We Mean When We Refer to the Deity of Jesus?

What Do We Mean When We Refer to the Deity of Jesus? Simply put, we are affirming that Jesus is God. More specifically, we are stating that Jesus is a person of the Trinity, co-equal with God the Father and God the Holy Spirit, and co-eternal, having existed with them from the beginning. This means that Jesus shares the same divine nature and attributes as the Father and the Spirit, emphasizing His full divinity and eternal existence.

The Athanasian Creed from Chapter 3 says it this way.

For this is the true faith that we believe and confess: That our Lord Jesus Christ, God's Son, is both God and man.
He is God, begotten before all worlds from the being of the Father, and he is man, born in the world from the being of his mother — existing fully as God, and fully as man with a rational soul and a human body; equal to the Father in divinity, subordinate to the Father in humanity.
Although he is God and man, he is not divided, but is one Christ.
He is united because God has taken humanity into himself; he does not transform deity into humanity.
He is completely one in the unity of his person, without confusing his natures.
For as the rational soul and body are one person, so the one Christ is God and man.

What Does the Bible Say?

When we thoroughly examine and study Scripture, it becomes clear that Jesus is God. The Bible explicitly states this in the opening verses of the Gospel of John:

"In the beginning the Word already existed. The Word was with God, and the Word was God. He existed in the beginning with God. God created everything through him, and nothing was created except through him. The Word gave life to everything that was created, and

his life brought light to everyone."
John 1:1-4 NLT

Through the inspiration of the Holy Spirit, John makes two profound declarations. First, he states that Jesus (referred to as "the Word") existed before creation and was with the Father, alluding to the Godhead. Second, John reveals that Jesus was not only with God as a distinct person but that He was simultaneously God. This is a profound and foundational truth of the Christian faith.

Throughout the Bible, additional passages affirm Jesus' divinity. To understand this fully, we will explore Scriptural evidence for the deity of Jesus. We will begin with Old Testament prophecies about the Messiah, then examine Jesus' own words, consider the beliefs of the disciples and apostles, and finally review the teachings of the early Church.

1. What did the Old Testament Prophets say?

Let's examine two Old Testament prophets, Isaiah and Jeremiah, and consider what they said about Jesus. In the first two passages, Isaiah speaks of the Messiah's (Jesus') birth and makes two significant claims: first, that He would be called "Immanuel" (God is with us), and second, that He would be called "Mighty God."

"All right then, the Lord himself will give you the sign. Look! The virgin will conceive a child! She will give birth to a son and will call him Immanuel (which means 'God is with us')."
Isaiah 7:14 NLT

"For a child is born to us, a son is given to us. The government will rest on his shoulders. And he will be called: Wonderful Counselor, Mighty God, Everlasting Father, Prince of Peace."
Isaiah 9:6 NLT

In the third passage from Isaiah, we see a prophecy that not only foretells the coming of Jesus but also references John the Baptist, who would prepare the way for Him. Notice the reference to John *"making the way for our God,"* connecting this passage with John 1:23:

"Listen! It's the voice of someone shouting, 'Clear the way through the wilderness for the Lord! Make a straight highway through the wasteland for our God!'"
Isaiah 40:3 NLT

Finally, Jeremiah 23:6 provides another powerful declaration of the Messiah's divine nature. Jeremiah refers to Him as *"The Lord Is Our Righteousness."* The word translated "Lord" here comes from the Hebrew Yahweh, later rendered as Jehovah, a name that exclusively refers to God.

"For the time is coming," says the Lord, "when I will raise up a righteous descendant from King David's line. He will be a King who rules with wisdom. He will do what is just and right throughout the land. And this will be his name: 'The Lord Is Our Righteousness.' In that day Judah will be saved, and Israel will live in safety."
Jeremiah 23:5-6 NLT

These prophecies from Isaiah and Jeremiah emphasize the divinity of Jesus, pointing to Him not just as a great leader or king but as God Himself, who came to dwell with His people and bring salvation.

2. What did Jesus say concerning himself?

You will not find a single passage in the Bible where Jesus explicitly states, "I am God." However, He made this claim in many different ways that were unmistakable to His audience. The challenge we face today lies in the cultural and linguistic gap between the modern reader and the context of Jesus' time. For those who were present with Him, His claims were clear, and they understood the profound significance of His words. Let's examine a few examples, starting with John 10:30:

"The Father and I are one."
John 10:30 NLT

At first glance, this statement may not seem significant to a modern reader, but to those present, it was a bold declaration of equality with God. Their response makes this clear—they picked up stones to kill Him, accusing Him of blasphemy: *"You, a mere man, claim to be God"* (John 10:33).

Another example can be found in John 8:58:

"Jesus answered, 'I tell you the truth, before Abraham was even born, I Am!'"
John 8:58 NLT

This statement also may seem innocent to modern readers, but His Jewish audience understood its meaning immediately. Jesus was claiming pre-existence and identifying Himself as Yahweh, the great "I AM" from Exodus 3:14. This declaration was seen as a direct claim to deity, which is why they attempted to stone Him for what they considered blasphemy (John 8:59; Leviticus 24:14).

Beyond Jesus' verbal claims, we also see instances where He was recognized and worshiped as God—and He accepted this worship without correction, which would have been unthinkable under Mosaic Law if He were not divine. Consider the following examples:

"My Lord and my God!" Thomas exclaimed.
John 20:28 NLT

"Then the disciples worshiped him. 'You really are the Son of God!' they exclaimed."
Matthew 14:33 NLT

"And as they went, Jesus met them and greeted them. And they ran to him, grasped his feet, and worshiped him."
Matthew 28:9 NLT

The disciples, as faithful Jews, were well aware of the Mosaic Law regarding blasphemy and its severe consequences. Yet they worshiped Jesus as God, and He accepted their worship as appropriate and true. This consistent pattern throughout the Gospels underscores the divinity of Jesus as both claimed by Him and recognized by His followers.

3. What did the disciples say concerning the deity of Jesus?

Through their time with Jesus—witnessing not only His miracles but also His character—the disciples became convinced that Jesus was the Messiah, the Son of God, and God incarnate. When He predicted His own death and resurrection and fulfilled it, their conviction was solidified, and their belief in Him became unshakable. This belief shaped the rest of their lives, many of which were cut short as a direct result of their unwavering faith. So, did the disciples believe that Jesus was God? Absolutely. Let's examine what they had to say.

The Apostle Paul declared:

"Abraham, Isaac, and Jacob are their ancestors, and Christ himself was an Israelite as far as his human nature is concerned. And he is God, the one who rules over everything and is worthy of eternal praise! Amen."
Romans 9:5 NLT

"Though he was God, he did not think of equality with God as something to cling to."
Philippians 2:6 NLT

The Apostle John affirmed Jesus' divinity:

"And we know that the Son of God has come, and he has given us understanding so that we can know the true God. And now we live in fellowship with the true God because we live in fellowship with his Son, Jesus Christ. He is the only true God, and he is eternal life."
1 John 5:20 NLT

Matthew's Gospel confirms the prophecy from Isaiah:

"All of this occurred to fulfill the Lord's message through his prophet: 'Look! The virgin will conceive a child! She will give birth to a son, and they will call him Immanuel, which means "God is with us."'"
Matthew 1:22-23 NLT

Let's not forget Thomas's declaration:

"My Lord and my God!" Thomas exclaimed.
John 20:28 NLT

The Apostle Peter also proclaimed Jesus' divinity:

"This letter is from Simon Peter, a slave and apostle of Jesus Christ. I am writing to you who share the same precious faith we have. This faith was given to you because of the justice and fairness of Jesus Christ, our God and Savior."
2 Peter 1:1 NLT

In Acts, Peter refers to Jesus as the "Author of Life":

"You killed the author of life, but God raised him from the dead. And we are witnesses of this fact!"
Acts 3:15 NLT

Beyond these Scriptural declarations, early church tradition teaches that many of the apostles were martyred for their belief in Jesus. Their willingness to die for their faith serves as a powerful testimony to their conviction that Jesus is God. Additionally, countless early Christians faced persecution and death for their belief in Jesus as the Messiah, further underscoring the profound impact of this truth.

What Did the Early Church Teach Concerning Jesus as God?

Polycarp (AD 69-155) was the bishop at the church in Smyrna. Irenaeus tells us Polycarp was a disciple of John the Apostle.

Now may the God and Father of our Lord Jesus Christ, and the eternal high priest himself, the Son of God Jesus Christ, build you up in faith and truth...and to us with you, and to all those under heaven who will yet believe in our Lord and God Jesus Christ and in his Father who raised him from the dead.

Ignatius (AD 50-117) was the bishop at the church in Antioch and also a disciple of John the Apostle. He wrote a series of letters to various churches on his way to Rome, where he was to be martyred.

Being as you are imitators of God, once you took on new life through the blood of God you completed perfectly the task so natural to you.

Justin Martyr (AD 100-165) was an Christian apologist of the second century.

Permit me first to recount the prophecies, which I wish to do in order to prove that Christ is called both God and Lord of hosts.

The Father of the universe has a Son; who also, being the first-begotten Word of God, is even God. And of old He appeared in the shape of fire and in the likeness of an angel to Moses and to the other prophets; but now in the times of your reign, having, as we before said, become Man by a virgin....

Melito of Sardis (died c. AD 180) was the bishop of the church in Sardis.

He that hung up the earth in space was Himself hanged up; He that fixed the heavens was fixed with nails; He that bore up the earth was born up on a tree; the Lord of all was subjected to ignominy in a naked body—God put to death! ... [I]n order that He might not be seen, the luminaries turned away, and the day became darkened—because they slew God, who hung naked on the tree....

The early Church Fathers strongly affirmed the deity of Jesus Christ in their writings, demonstrating that this belief was central to early Christian theology. Polycarp, a disciple of John the Apostle, referred to Jesus as "our Lord and God," emphasizing His divine nature alongside the Father. Ignatius of Antioch, also a disciple of John, described salvation as being made possible through "the blood of God," further affirming Jesus' divine identity. Justin Martyr, a second-century Christian apologist, explicitly stated that Jesus is both "God and Lord of hosts" and identified Him as the eternal Word of God, preexistent and active in Old Testament events. Melito of Sardis poetically described Jesus as the Creator who was crucified, declaring that "God was put to death" for the redemption of humanity. These testimonies from early Church leaders illustrate the unwavering belief in Jesus' divinity, rooted in apostolic teaching and foundational to the faith of the early Church.

What Divine Attributes Did Jesus Possess?

When considering the deity of Jesus, it's important not only to examine identity statements but also to explore His attributes. If Jesus were merely human, He would have been limited in ability, just like any other person. However, if He is truly God, His divine nature would be evident in His qualities. Beyond His recorded miracles, Scripture attributes the following divine characteristics to Jesus:

1. Jesus being eternal.

"Now, Father, bring me into the glory we shared before the world began."
John 17:5 NLT

"He existed before anything else, and he holds all creation together."
Colossians 1:17 NLT

2. Jesus being omnipresent.

"For where two or three gather together as my followers, I am there among them.""
Matthew 18:20 NLT

"Teach these new disciples to obey all the commands I have given you. And be sure of this: I am with you always, even to the end of the age.""
Matthew 28:20 NLT

3. Jesus being omniscient

"No one needed to tell him about human nature, for he knew what was in each person's heart."
John 2:25 NLT

"Now we understand that you know everything, and there's no need to question you. From this we believe that you came from God.""
John 16:30 NLT

4. Jesus being omnipotent

"Jesus came and told his disciples, "I have been given all authority in heaven and on earth."
Matthew 28:18 NLT

"He will take our weak mortal bodies and change them into glorious bodies like his own, using the same power with which he will bring everything under his control."
Philippians 3:21 NLT

5. Jesus being immutable.

"He also says to the Son, "In the beginning, Lord, you laid the foundation of the earth and made the heavens with your hands. They will perish, but you remain forever. They will wear out like old clothing. You will fold them up like a cloak and discard them like old clothing. But you are always the same; you will live forever.""
Hebrews 1:10-12 NLT

"Jesus Christ is the same yesterday, today, and forever."
Hebrews 13:8 NLT

Why Does It Matter?

The short answer is this: if Jesus were not God, He could not have died for our sins. No mere human could bear and fully satisfy the infinite wrath of God. The satisfaction of God's wrath required a sacrifice of immeasurable value—something only Christ, as God, could provide. Through His divine nature, Jesus bore the sins of the world, satisfied the judgment of God the Father, and conquered death once and for all.

Prophecies foretold that the coming Messiah would be God. Jesus Himself claimed divinity, the apostles affirmed this belief through their words and actions, and the early Church taught this truth from the beginning. When we examine His life, we see the attributes of His divine nature, reflecting the very nature of God. For me, this foundational truth is undeniable.

Further Study

1. What does the term "deity of Jesus" mean, and why is it a foundational doctrine of Christianity?
2. Which biblical passages explicitly affirm the deity of Jesus, such as John 1:1, Colossians 1:15-20, and Hebrews 1:1-4, and how do they support this belief?
3. How did Jesus Himself claim to be divine, and what were the reactions of His contemporaries to these claims? (e.g., John 8:58, Mark 2:5-7)
4. How does Jesus' deity impact our understanding of the incarnation and His role as both fully God and fully man?
5. Why is the deity of Jesus essential for the Christian understanding of salvation and His ability to atone for the sins of humanity?
6. How did the early Church defend the deity of Jesus against heresies such as Arianism, and what role did the Council of Nicaea play in affirming this doctrine?

Additional Notes:

5. Human Depravity

Key Terms

1. **Depravity** - The moral and spiritual corruption of humanity due to sin, rendering people incapable of pleasing God on their own (Romans 3:10-12; Jeremiah 17:9).
2. **Original Sin** - The doctrine that all humanity inherits a sinful nature and guilt from Adam's disobedience in the Garden of Eden (Genesis 3; Romans 5:12-19).
3. **Total Depravity** - The belief that every aspect of human nature—mind, will, and emotions—has been corrupted by sin, leaving humanity unable to seek or respond to God without His grace (Ephesians 2:1-3; Isaiah 64:6).
4. **Sin Nature** - The inherent inclination toward sin that all humans possess as a result of the Fall (Psalm 51:5; Romans 7:18-20).
5. **Spiritual Death** - The separation from God caused by sin, resulting in humanity's inability to have a right relationship with Him apart from Christ (Ephesians 2:1; Colossians 2:13).
6. **Grace** - God's unmerited favor that enables salvation and transformation, countering the effects of human depravity through His mercy and love (Ephesians 2:8-9; Titus 2:11).

What is human depravity?

Human Depravity is the doctrine that teaches humanity, since the Fall, has inherited both the guilt and sin nature of Adam. This inheritance affects every part of human existence, including the mind, will, emotions, and body. Often referred to as "total depravity," "total inability," "righteous incapability," "radical corruption," or "moral inability," the key issue is not the terminology but how accurately the doctrine reflects the Bible's teaching about the spiritual condition of fallen humanity.

There are three primary perspectives on human depravity:

1. **Arminianism: Partial Depravity**
   Arminianism teaches that humanity is depraved but still has the ability to seek God. While humans are fallen and tainted by sin, they are not so corrupted that they cannot choose to come to God and accept salvation, provided they receive prevenient grace from God. This grace enables free will, allowing individuals to yield to the influence of the Holy Spirit.
2. **Calvinism: Total Depravity**
   Calvinism holds that humanity is completely depraved and utterly unable to seek God on its own. Sin has so thoroughly corrupted human nature that individuals cannot choose to come to God or accept salvation without God's irresistible grace. When this grace is extended, human will is powerless to resist the transformative influence of the Holy Spirit.
3. **Pelagianism: Heresy**
   Pelagianism is the unbiblical teaching that Adam's sin did not affect future generations. According to this view, Adam's sin was solely his own, and his descendants did not inherit a sinful nature. Pelagianism claims that every human soul is created directly by God and begins in a state of innocence, free from sin. It asserts that humans are not inherently sinful but are instead

fundamentally good. This teaching has been condemned as heresy by the Church.

What is it not?

The Doctrine of Human Depravity does not claim that sinners are as bad as they could possibly be, nor does it imply that any individual is entirely evil or incapable of doing good. It also does not mean that fallen humans lack a conscience or that the world, since the Fall, is devoid of joy, progress, or the ability to appreciate beauty and goodness. Despite the prevalent effects of sin, people can still perform acts of kindness, compassion, generosity, and justice—what we might call civil or relational goodness.

This capacity for goodness is attributed to God's common grace. Through the work of the Holy Spirit, God restrains the full expression of humanity's sinful nature and the potential flood of wickedness from the human heart. At the same time, He enables individuals to pursue and carry out deeds that reflect His image, even in a fallen world. Without this divine restraint and influence, human society would descend into chaos and moral decay. Common grace ensures that humanity, though fallen, can still experience moments of goodness and beauty that point back to God's character.

Was it always this way?

It wasn't always this way. At the beginning of creation, sin had not yet entered the world. Humans were made in the image of God, reflecting His holiness and being set apart for His purposes. This is evident in the following passage from Genesis:

"Then God said, "Let us make human beings in our image, to be like us. They will reign over the fish in the sea, the birds in the sky, the livestock, all the wild animals on the earth, and the small animals that scurry along the ground." So God created human beings in his own

image. In the image of God he created them; male and female he created them."
Genesis 1:26-27 NLT

However, humanity's current state of depravity was not God's original intent. This corruption began with the sin of Adam and Eve, as described in Genesis:

"The woman was convinced. She saw that the tree was beautiful and its fruit looked delicious, and she wanted the wisdom it would give her. So she took some of the fruit and ate it. Then she gave some to her husband, who was with her, and he ate it, too. At that moment their eyes were opened, and they suddenly felt shame at their nakedness. So they sewed fig leaves together to cover themselves."
Genesis 3:6-7 NLT

The choice Adam and Eve made in the garden introduced humanity's sinful condition, referred to as "original sin." The doctrine of Original Sin teaches that all people inherit Adam's guilt and sinful nature through natural generation. This is why Jesus, who was born of a virgin, was free from this inherited sin. Together with Adam's imputed condemnation, we are all born guilty before God. Original Sin explains that we sin because we are inherently sinners (Romans 3:23), entering the world with a corrupt nature and without hope apart from the saving grace of God through the gospel. The Apostle Paul addresses this in his letter to the Romans:

"When Adam sinned, sin entered the world. Adam's sin brought death, so death spread to everyone, for everyone sinned. Yes, people sinned even before the law was given. But it was not counted as sin because there was not yet any law to break. Still, everyone died—from the time of Adam to the time of Moses—even those who did not disobey an explicit commandment of God, as Adam did. Now Adam is a symbol, a representation of Christ, who was yet to come. But there is a great difference between Adam's sin and God's gracious gift. For the sin of this one man, Adam, brought death to many. But even greater is God's

wonderful grace and his gift of forgiveness to many through this other man, Jesus Christ."
Romans 5:12-15 NLT

This passage clearly shows that one man's sin resulted in the inherent sin nature of every man, woman, and child—human depravity. Paul further explains this condition in Romans chapter 7:

"So the trouble is not with the law, for it is spiritual and good. The trouble is with me, for I am all too human, a slave to sin. I don't really understand myself, for I want to do what is right, but I don't do it. Instead, I do what I hate. But if I know that what I am doing is wrong, this shows that I agree that the law is good. So I am not the one doing wrong; it is sin living in me that does it. And I know that nothing good lives in me, that is, in my sinful nature. I want to do what is right, but I can't."
Romans 7:14-18 NLT

These passages reveal that humanity's sinful condition began with Adam's disobedience, leaving us in desperate need of God's saving grace through Jesus Christ.

What Did Jesus Teach?

One of the great misconceptions in the Church today is the belief that Jesus is content with everyone staying just as they are—that there's no need to change, surrender, or bear a cross because Jesus is merely a "buddy" figure. But is this what Scripture reveals? When we examine Jesus' life and teachings, nothing could be further from the truth. Everyone was welcome at His table, but Jesus clearly called people to lay down their old ways and embrace a new way of living. This call to transformation stems from the reality of humanity's brokenness. Jesus desired for us to recognize our sinful nature and turn from it in full surrender to Him.

In the Sermon on the Mount, Jesus taught that even the best human intentions are marred by sin. While discussing prayer in Matthew 7:11, He refers to people as "sinful" (translated from the Greek word *ponērós*, meaning evil, bad, or wicked). One definition even describes it as the negative moral quality of being opposed to God and His goodness. Though His primary point was to highlight the generosity of God, Jesus' statement also underscores humanity's inherent depravity: even those who give "good gifts" are fundamentally sinful.

"So if you sinful people know how to give good gifts to your children, how much more will your heavenly Father give good gifts to those who ask him."
Matthew 7:11 NLT

In the Gospel of Mark, Jesus addresses Jewish rituals of purity and makes a profound statement about the source of sin. He explains that defilement doesn't come from external factors but from the internal condition of the human heart. Every aspect of the human condition—body, soul, and mind—is tainted by sin.

"And then he added, 'It is what comes from inside that defiles you. For from within, out of a person's heart, come evil thoughts, sexual immorality, theft, murder, adultery, greed, wickedness, deceit, lustful desires, envy, slander, pride, and foolishness. All these vile things come from within; they are what defile you.'"
Mark 7:20-23 NLT

This theme runs consistently throughout the Gospels. Jesus commends the tax collector in Luke 18:9-14 for his humble acknowledgment of being a sinner. In Luke 7, Jesus teaches that all humans are morally indebted to God. And throughout His ministry, He calls everyone to repent of their sins and turn back to God. Jesus confirmed the universal sinfulness of humanity and established forgiveness as the central purpose of His ministry and sacrifice.

Why does it matter?

Humanity often seeks affirmation of its self-worth, innate goodness, and importance, desiring to be encouraged, coddled, and reassured of its value. However, the doctrine of human depravity dismantles this self-centered perspective. Rather than portraying humanity as deserving or entitled to God's love and mercy, it reveals a far harsher reality: we are not only undeserving but are, in fact, worthy of God's eternal wrath due to the depth of our sinfulness.

Fully understanding our condition is essential for grasping the magnitude of God's grace and the significance of our salvation. Without this awareness, we risk minimizing the cost of redemption and the extraordinary nature of God's mercy. Human depravity affects every aspect of our being—our thoughts, emotions, actions, and motivations—leaving nothing untouched by sin. As Isaiah declares, *"...all our righteous acts are like filthy rags"* before a holy and perfect God. Even our best efforts fall hopelessly short of His standard of righteousness.

This sobering truth forces us to confront the depth of our need for divine grace. Only when we recognize our total inability to save ourselves can we fully appreciate the gift of salvation offered through Jesus Christ. It is in the light of this understanding that God's mercy, love, and forgiveness shine most brightly.

"We are all infected and impure with sin. When we display our righteous deeds, they are nothing but filthy rags. Like autumn leaves, we wither and fall, and our sins sweep us away like the wind."
Isaiah 64:6 NLT

"Once you were dead because of your disobedience and your many sins. You used to live in sin, just like the rest of the world, obeying the devil—the commander of the powers in the unseen world. He is the spirit at work in the hearts of those who refuse to obey God. All of us used to live that way, following the passionate desires and inclinations

*of our sinful nature. By our very nature we were subject to God's
anger, just like everyone else."*
Ephesians 2:1-3 NLT

*"Well then, should we conclude that we Jews are better than others?
No, not at all, for we have already shown that all people, whether Jews
or Gentiles, are under the power of sin. As the Scriptures say, "No one
is righteous— not even one. No one is truly wise; no one is seeking God.
All have turned away; all have become useless. No one does good, not a
single one." "Their talk is foul, like the stench from an open grave. Their
tongues are filled with lies." "Snake venom drips from their lips." "Their
mouths are full of cursing and bitterness." "They rush to commit
murder. Destruction and misery always follow them. They don't know
where to find peace." "They have no fear of God at all." Obviously, the
law applies to those to whom it was given, for its purpose is to keep
people from having excuses, and to show that the entire world is guilty
before God. For no one can ever be made right with God by doing what
the law commands. The law simply shows us how sinful we are."*
Romans 3:9-20 NLT

Fully understanding this doctrine brings us to the humbling
realization that we cannot earn God's love, mercy, or forgiveness. It
teaches us that we cannot "buy" our way into heaven with good works
but must rely fully on faith and grace. This understanding helps us
address difficult questions like, "Why would a loving God send 'good'
people to hell?" and "Why do bad things happen to 'good' people?" The
reality is that the broken condition of our world is not the result of God's
actions but a consequence of humanity's disobedience and sin.

This doctrine not only reveals who we are but also reveals who
God is. Despite our sinful condition, God chose to reveal Himself to us
and provide a way for us to be made righteous and saved. When we were
hopeless, God intervened. The Apostle Paul makes it abundantly clear
that there is an answer to the problem of sin and human depravity—and
that answer is Jesus Christ.

"Oh, what a miserable person I am! Who will free me from this life that is dominated by sin and death? Thank God! The answer is in Jesus Christ our Lord. So you see how it is: In my mind I really want to obey God's law, but because of my sinful nature I am a slave to sin."
Romans 7:24-25 NLT

He doubles down on that sentiment in the beginning verses of chapter 8.

"So now there is no condemnation for those who belong to Christ Jesus. And because you belong to him, the power of the life-giving Spirit has freed you from the power of sin that leads to death."
Romans 8:1-2 NLT

The doctrine of Human Depravity swiftly confronts and dispels the falsehoods and lies the enemy uses to downplay our sinful condition. It also dismantles the incorrect notion that we can earn eternal life with Jesus through our own efforts or good works. Ultimately, this doctrine leads us to the profound truth that our only hope is found in Jesus Christ.

"In fact, it says, "The message is very close at hand; it is on your lips and in your heart." And that message is the very message about faith that we preach: If you openly declare that Jesus is Lord and believe in your heart that God raised him from the dead, you will be saved. For it is by believing in your heart that you are made right with God, and it is by openly declaring your faith that you are saved. As the Scriptures tell us, "Anyone who trusts in him will never be disgraced." Jew and Gentile are the same in this respect. They have the same Lord, who gives generously to all who call on him. For "Everyone who calls on the name of the Lord will be saved.""
Romans 10:8-13 NLT

Further Study

1. What is the doctrine of human depravity, and how does it describe the spiritual condition of humanity apart from God?
2. Which biblical passages, such as Romans 3:10-12 and Jeremiah 17:9, emphasize the sinful nature of humanity, and how do they shape our understanding of depravity?
3. How does human depravity affect our ability to seek God, understand spiritual truths, and live righteously on our own?
4. What is the difference between total depravity and utter depravity, and how does this distinction clarify the extent of humanity's fallen nature?
5. How does the doctrine of human depravity underscore the necessity of God's grace and the work of Christ in salvation?
6. In what ways does understanding human depravity deepen our appreciation for God's mercy and the transformative power of the Holy Spirit?

Look at additional Biblical texts that affirm the depravity of the human heart, for example Genesis 6:5; 8:21; Job 15:14-16; Psalm 14:2-3; 51:5; 58:3; Proverbs 22:15; Jeremiah 13:23; 17:9; Matthew 7:15-20; John 3:6; 6:44;

- Original Sin: Original sin means that all mankind enters into life with a fallen human nature that leaves us dead in our trespasses and sin. We're not sinners because we sin; we sin because we are sinners.

- Imputed Sin: Imputed sin deals with the fact that the guilt of Adam is credited not just to Adam himself, but also to all humanity. This doesn't mean we are personally guilty of Adam's sin (we're not) but that his sin was credited to us like into our account or ledger. In this way all of us, except Christ, who was born of a virgin, are regarded as having sinned in the first Adam and share in his guilt.

- Imputed Righteousness: Imputed righteousness deals with the fact that the righteousness of Jesus has been credited to us through His sacrifice. It means we have a right standing or right positioning with God as a result of what he's done. We need the righteousness of Christ imputed to us because we have no righteousness of our own. We are sinners by nature, and we cannot make ourselves righteous—we cannot place ourselves in right standing with God. We need Christ's righteousness imputed to us—meaning, we need His holiness before God credited to our account.

Additional Notes:

6. Jesus' Virgin Conception

Key Terms

1. **Virgin Birth** -: The miraculous event in which Jesus was conceived by the Holy Spirit and born of the Virgin Mary, fulfilling prophecy and affirming His divine origin (Matthew 1:18-25; Luke 1:26-38).
2. **Immaculate Conception** -: Often confused with the virgin conception, this term specifically refers to the Roman Catholic belief that Mary was conceived without original sin to prepare her to be the mother of Jesus. It is distinct from Jesus' virgin conception.
3. **Incarnation** - The theological term for the event in which God the Son took on human nature and was born as Jesus, fully God and fully man (John 1:14; Philippians 2:6-8).
4. **Holy Spirit** - The third Person of the Trinity who caused the miraculous conception of Jesus in Mary's womb, emphasizing divine intervention (Luke 1:35).
5. **Prophecy** - The foretelling of future events by divine inspiration. Jesus' virgin conception fulfilled prophecies such as Isaiah 7:14, which declared that a virgin would bear a son called Immanuel.
6. **Messiah** - The promised Savior and Redeemer of humanity. Jesus' virgin conception signifies His unique role as the Messiah, born without sin to save His people (Matthew 1:21-23).

The virgin conception, often referred to as the virgin birth, should not be confused with the Catholic doctrine of the Immaculate Conception. The Catholic Church teaches that from the very moment of her conception, the Virgin Mary was free from the stain of original sin. This means she was in a state of grace from the beginning, sharing in God's divine life, and was free from the sinful inclinations that have affected human nature since the Fall. However, this doctrine has no basis in Scripture.

The concept of the Immaculate Conception originated in the Eastern Church during the seventh century and later spread to the Western Church in the eighth century. By the 11th century, it had been named the Immaculate Conception. In the 18th century, it was officially defined as a dogma of the Catholic Church and established as a feast day celebrated universally.

"For everyone has sinned; we all fall short of God's glorious standard."
Romans 3:23 NLT

What does the Virgin Conception Imply?

The virgin conception of Jesus teaches that He was born apart from the normal process of procreation. Instead, He was supernaturally conceived in the womb of the Virgin Mary by the power of the Holy Spirit and born of her without sin. This miraculous event highlights the divine origin of Jesus and ensures His sinless nature, setting Him apart from all humanity. The clearest biblical teachings on the virgin conception are found in the Gospels of Matthew and Luke, the only two places in Scripture where the birth of Christ is narrated. It is significant that both accounts emphasize the virginity of Mary and the role of the Holy Spirit in Jesus' conception.

"This is how Jesus the Messiah was born. His mother, Mary, was engaged to be married to Joseph. But before the marriage took place, while she was still a virgin, she became pregnant through the power of the Holy Spirit."
Matthew 1:18 NLT

"Mary asked the angel, 'But how can this happen? I am a virgin.' The angel replied, 'The Holy Spirit will come upon you, and the power of the Most High will overshadow you. So the baby to be born will be holy, and he will be called the Son of God.'"
Luke 1:34-35 NLT

This event was a miraculous intervention by God, bringing about the conception of Christ without a human father. No man or angel was involved in this process. Christ, who is God from all eternity, united Himself with human nature through this miraculous conception, taking on flesh and dwelling among us. This truth underscores the mystery of the Incarnation, where the eternal Son of God became fully human while remaining fully divine.

The Virgin Birth in Church History

Historically, the virgin birth has been regarded as an essential doctrine of the Christian faith. This belief is affirmed in the amended version of the Nicene Creed from 381 AD, which states:

"For us men and for our salvation, he came down from heaven, and by the Holy Spirit was incarnate of the Virgin Mary, and became man."

Similarly, the Apostle's Creed affirms:

"I believe in God, the Father almighty, Creator of heaven and earth, and in Jesus Christ, his only Son, our Lord, who was conceived by the Holy Spirit, born of the Virgin Mary..."

These statements show that the doctrine of the virgin birth has deep roots in the early Church, becoming a cornerstone of Christian orthodoxy.

Additionally, early Church leaders also emphasized this doctrine. Ignatius of Antioch, writing as early as AD 110–117, mentioned the virgin birth on several occasions. Born in Syria around AD 35, Ignatius is believed to have been a disciple of the Apostle John. He later became the bishop of Antioch and a significant figure in the early Christian Church. His writings offer important insights into the beliefs and theology of the time. Among his mentions of the virgin birth is the following passage:

Ignatius' Epistle to the Magnesians

"I desire to guard you beforehand, that ye fall not upon the hooks of vain doctrine, but that you may rather attain to a full assurance in Christ, who was begotten by the Father before all ages, but was afterwards born of the Virgin Mary without any intercourse with man."

The second-century church fathers Aristides of Athens (A.D. 138), Justin Martyr (A.D. 165), Melito of Sardis (A.D. 170), and Irenaeus of Lyons (A.D. 180) all affirm the virgin birth as well.

The Apology of Aristides

"The Christians, then, trace the beginning of their religion from Jesus the Messiah; and he is named the Son of GodMost High. And it is said that God came down from heaven, and from a Hebrew virgin assumed and clothed himself with flesh; and the Son of God lived in a daughter of man."

Melito of Sardis

"For the sake of suffering humanity he came down from heaven to earth, clothed himself in that humanity in the Virgin's womb, and was born a man."

Justin Martyr's Dialogue with Trypho

"And I, resuming the discourse where I had left off at a previous stage, when proving that He was born of a virgin, and that His birth of a virgin had been predicted by Isaiah."

Irenaeus' Against Heresies

"Christ Jesus, the Son of God, because of His surpassing love towards his creation, humbled himself to be born of the virgin. Thereby, He united man through Himself to God."

Why Is It Significant and Why Does It Matter?

One of the greatest significances of the virgin conception is that it fulfills one of over 300 prophecies about Jesus, affirming both the validity of Scripture and the divine nature of Christ. To undermine the virgin conception is to undermine the reliability of the Bible and the identity of Jesus, which is why it is often targeted by movements such as deconstructionism. The prophecy is found in Isaiah 7:14, given by the prophet Isaiah approximately 700 years before the birth of Jesus:

"All right then, the Lord himself will give you the sign. Look! The virgin will conceive a child! She will give birth to a son and will call him Immanuel (which means 'God is with us')."
Isaiah 7:14 NLT

The fulfillment of this prophecy is recorded in the Gospel of Matthew:

"All of this occurred to fulfill the Lord's message through his prophet: 'Look! The virgin will conceive a child! She will give birth to a son, and they will call him Immanuel, which means "God is with us."'"
Matthew 1:22-23 NLT

God's people were prepared to expect a Messiah born through a miraculous, supernatural event—a virgin conception and birth. This truth explains how Jesus could be both fully God and fully human. He received His humanity from His mother, Mary, and His divinity from God the Father. If Jesus were not born of a virgin, questions about His parentage would compromise the Gospel. The virgin birth is foundational for understanding how Jesus is both God and man, how He remained without sin, and how salvation is entirely a work of God's grace. If Jesus were not born of a virgin, He would have had a human father, undermining His divinity and rendering the Bible untrue.

The virgin birth confirms that our Redeemer is fully human—yet without sin. Every human birth, since Adam, has resulted in a sinner because Adam's sin corrupted the human race. To be the perfect substitute for humanity, our Savior had to be genuinely human and entirely sinless to bear our guilt and pay the penalty for our sins. Paul explains this in Romans:

"But there is a great difference between Adam's sin and God's gracious gift. For the sin of this one man, Adam, brought death to many. But even greater is God's wonderful grace and his gift of forgiveness to many through this other man, Jesus Christ. And the result of God's gracious gift is very different from the result of that one man's sin. For Adam's sin led to condemnation, but God's free gift leads to our being made right with God, even though we are guilty of many sins. For the sin of this one man, Adam, caused death to rule over many. But even greater is God's wonderful grace and his gift of righteousness, for all who receive it will live in triumph over sin and death through this one man, Jesus Christ."
Romans 5:15-17 NLT

The virgin birth also affirms the preexistent, divine sonship of Jesus. As discussed in chapter 3, the members of the Trinity—Father, Son, and Holy Spirit—are co-equal and co-eternal. Jesus existed long before His incarnation. The virgin birth is therefore fitting for the one who was already the Son of God before entering the world. He is uniquely the God-man, the only one capable of accomplishing salvation. He is Immanuel—God with us.

Additionally, the virgin birth highlights God's initiative in salvation. Salvation is a gift that humanity could never achieve on its own. Before the incarnation, countless attempts were made to achieve lasting salvation, but only God's plan, executed in His perfect timing and way, could accomplish it. The virgin birth contrasts God's power with humanity's powerlessness to bring about true redemption.

To reiterate, without the virgin birth, there is no salvation for sinners. Without it, Jesus Christ would be a sinful human being, and the Bible would be untrustworthy. The virgin birth is an essential component of salvation and the truth of Scripture. As the church father

Irenaeus aptly stated, *"If one does not accept [the Son of God's] birth from a Virgin, how can he accept His resurrection from the dead?"*

Further Study

1. What does the Bible teach about the virgin conception of Jesus, and which passages explicitly describe this event? (e.g., Matthew 1:18-25, Luke 1:26-38)
2. Why is the virgin conception significant in affirming Jesus' divine nature and His identity as the Son of God?
3. How does the virgin conception fulfill Old Testament prophecy, particularly Isaiah 7:14, and what does this reveal about God's redemptive plan?
4. What role did the Holy Spirit play in the virgin conception, and how does this demonstrate God's supernatural intervention in human history?
5. How does the virgin conception safeguard the sinlessness of Jesus and His ability to serve as the perfect sacrifice for sin?
6. What are some common objections to the virgin conception, and how can Christians respond to these challenges from a biblical and theological perspective?

Additional Notes:

7. Jesus' Sinlessness

Key Terms

1. **Sinlessness** - The attribute of Jesus Christ being completely free from sin in thought, word, and deed, making Him the perfect Lamb of God (Hebrews 4:15; 1 Peter 2:22).
2. **Impeccability** - The doctrine that Jesus was not only sinless but incapable of sinning because of His divine nature, ensuring His moral perfection (2 Corinthians 5:21; John 8:46).
3. **Temptation** - The trials Jesus faced during His earthly life, including direct confrontation with Satan, through which He remained sinless and obedient to God's will (Matthew 4:1-11; Hebrews 2:18).
4. **Atonement** - The reconciliation between God and humanity accomplished through Jesus' sacrificial death. His sinlessness qualified Him to be the perfect substitute for sinful humanity (1 John 2:2; Romans 5:9).
5. **High Priest** - A title for Jesus emphasizing His role in mediating between God and humanity. His sinlessness allows Him to intercede on our behalf effectively (Hebrews 7:26-27; Hebrews 4:14-15).
6. **Holiness** - The quality of being completely pure and set apart from sin. Jesus' holiness reflects His divine nature and perfect obedience to the Father (Luke 1:35; John 17:19).

The sinlessness of Jesus is an essential part of the doctrine of salvation. While it is not necessary to fully grasp this concept to be saved, it is essential to the work of the cross. If Jesus had been sinful, He would have been unable to pay the debt of sin on humanity's behalf. Just as sin entered the world through one man, Adam, God redeemed the world through one man, Jesus Christ. The Apostle Paul records this truth in his letter to the church in Rome:

"For the sin of this one man, Adam, caused death to rule over many. But even greater is God's wonderful grace and his gift of righteousness, for all who receive it will live in triumph over sin and death through this one man, Jesus Christ."
Romans 5:17 NLT

Christ's sinless life is set against the backdrop of Scripture's testimony to the depravity of man (see Chapter 5). This stark contrast highlights Jesus' unique nature and mission. Scripture consistently affirms the sinful condition of humanity, as seen in the words of Job, the acknowledgment of Solomon, and the testimony of John. Even the Apostle Paul emphasizes that *"everyone has sinned"*:

"Look, God does not even trust the angels. Even the heavens are not absolutely pure in his sight. How much less pure is a corrupt and sinful person with a thirst for wickedness!"
Job 15:15-16 NLT

"If they sin against you—and who has never sinned?—you might become angry with them and let their enemies conquer them and take them captive to their land far away or near."
1 Kings 8:46 NLT

"If we claim we have no sin, we are only fooling ourselves and not living in the truth."
1 John 1:8 NLT

"For everyone has sinned; we all fall short of God's glorious standard."
Romans 3:23 NLT

Time and time again, Scripture and daily experience remind us of humanity's fallen nature. In light of this universal truth, a critical question arises: Was Jesus, who was fully human, actually sinless? This question is central to understanding the unique role of Christ in God's redemptive plan, as His sinlessness qualifies Him to be the perfect sacrifice for our sins and the source of our righteousness.

Was Jesus Sinless?

Yes, Jesus was sinless, and it is because of His sinlessness that we have the hope of eternity in heaven. Jesus is referred to as the "Lamb of God," a title proclaimed by John the Baptist (John 1:29, 36). This title identifies Jesus as the perfect and ultimate sacrifice for sin, fulfilling the prophecy in Isaiah 53. According to Old Testament law, sacrificial lambs had to be spotless and without defect. As the "Lamb of God," Jesus met these qualifications perfectly. His sinlessness was not only a theological necessity but also the foundation of His role as our Savior.

In the New Testament, this concept is further explained. Paul highlights in Colossians 2 how the Old Testament laws and sacrificial system pointed forward to Christ's ultimate sacrifice on the cross. Jesus' death fulfilled the requirements of the law and offered final atonement for sin, freeing believers from its power:

"For these rules are only shadows of the reality yet to come. And Christ himself is that reality."
Colossians 2:17 NLT

The Apostle John also emphasizes Jesus' sinlessness and His mission to take away our sins:

"Everyone who sins is breaking God's law, for all sin is contrary to the law of God. And you know that Jesus came to take away our sins, and

there is no sin in him."
1 John 3:4-5 NLT

One of the most striking moments in Jesus' ministry occurs when He challenges a crowd to examine Him and point out any sin in His life. Of course, no one could accuse Him of wrongdoing. Imagine asking such a question of yourself today—most of us would be met with a flood of accusations highlighting our shortcomings. Yet Jesus, being sinless, was met with silence.

"So when I tell the truth, you just naturally don't believe me! Which of you can truthfully accuse me of sin? And since I am telling you the truth, why don't you believe me?"
John 8:45-46 NLT

As the sacrificial "Lamb of God," Jesus needed to remain spotless, and the Gospels confirm that He did so, even to the end. Pilate, after a thorough examination, could find no guilt in Him. In fact, all four Gospels record that Pilate declares Jesus innocent, yet He was still sentenced to death at the insistence of the crowd:

""Why?" Pilate demanded. "What crime has he committed?" But the mob roared even louder, "Crucify him!""
Matthew 27:23 NLT

""Why?" Pilate demanded. "What crime has he committed?" But the mob roared even louder, "Crucify him!""
Mark 15:14 NLT

"Then Pilate called together the leading priests and other religious leaders, along with the people, and he announced his verdict. "You brought this man to me, accusing him of leading a revolt. I have examined him thoroughly on this point in your presence and find him innocent. Herod came to the same conclusion and sent him back to us. Nothing this man has done calls for the death penalty.""
Luke 23:13-15 NLT

"When they saw him, the leading priests and Temple guards began shouting, "Crucify him! Crucify him!" "Take him yourselves and crucify him," Pilate said. "I find him not guilty.""
John 19:6 NLT

The sinlessness of Jesus is foundational to His role as Savior. Without His perfect, spotless nature, He could not have fulfilled the requirements necessary to be the final and sufficient sacrifice for our sins. According to God's standard, only a pure, unblemished offering could atone for sin, and Jesus met this standard perfectly through His life of complete obedience and righteousness. His perfection ensured that He was uniquely qualified to bear the full weight of humanity's sin on the cross, satisfying the justice of a holy God.

Because of His sinlessness, we can have absolute assurance in the hope of forgiveness, redemption, and eternal life. His flawless sacrifice means that the debt of sin has been paid in full, making salvation available to all who trust in Him. The sinlessness of Jesus not only secures our salvation but also stands as a reminder of His divine nature and the incredible love He demonstrated through His willingness to die in our place.

How Could Jesus Be Sinless?

So how could Jesus be sinless? He was fully God, but also fully man, and as we learned in Lesson 5, all people are depraved and sinful. While this is true for humanity, the answer lies in the previous lesson on the Doctrine of the Virgin Conception. Let's consider Romans 5:12:

"When Adam sinned, sin entered the world. Adam's sin brought death, so death spread to everyone, for everyone sinned."
Romans 5:12 NLT

Through Adam, sin was passed down from generation to generation, affecting all humankind to this very day. However, Jesus was not born through natural conception and, therefore, did not inherit the curse of sin. Notice carefully that Romans 5:12 specifies, *"When Adam sinned, sin entered the world,"* and that death spread to *"everyone."* The verse does not attribute the entrance of sin to both Adam and Eve. Sin entered the world through Adam, not Eve, and it was Adam who passed the curse of sin onto his descendants.

This understanding aligns with Genesis 3:15, where God promises that the One who will crush Satan will come from the *offspring of a woman,* not a man:

"And I will cause hostility between you and the woman, and between your offspring and her offspring. He will strike your head, and you will strike his heel."
Genesis 3:15 NLT

The New King James Version uses the term *"seed"* for additional clarity:

"And I will put enmity between you and the woman, and between your seed and her Seed; He shall bruise your head, and you shall bruise His heel."
Genesis 3:15 NKJV

It is a known biological fact that certain traits, disorders, and diseases can be transmitted exclusively by either the father or the mother. Similarly, it is possible that the sin nature (the inherent power of sin, not individual acts of sin) is passed down through the father. In the case of Jesus, His miraculous conception by the power of the Holy Spirit ensured that God, not a human man, was His Father. This prevented Him from inheriting the sin nature.

This explanation also addresses the false teaching of the Immaculate Conception, which claims that Mary had to be sinless for Jesus to be born without sin. Scripture does not support this idea. As a woman, Mary's sin nature would not have been passed down to Jesus. Instead, through the miraculous intervention of the Holy Spirit, Jesus was born free of the sin inherited by the rest of humanity.

Could Jesus be tempted?

Could Jesus be tempted? Scripture makes it clear that He could and indeed was tempted. However, to be tempted is not sinful in itself. The writer of Hebrews emphasizes this truth about Christ:

"So then, since we have a great High Priest who has entered heaven, Jesus the Son of God, let us hold firmly to what we believe. This High Priest of ours understands our weaknesses, for he faced all of the same testings we do, yet he did not sin."
Hebrews 4:14-15 NLT

Jesus remained sinless throughout His time on Earth, demonstrating His victory over the constant temptations of this world. This victory is most vividly seen in His direct confrontation with Satan when He was led into the wilderness by the Holy Spirit:

"Then Jesus was led by the Spirit into the wilderness to be tempted there by the devil. Then the devil went away, and angels came and took care of Jesus."
Matthew 4:1 NLT

Where Adam and Eve failed in the face of temptation, Jesus succeeded. He remained innocent, or "spotless," revealing both His divine nature and His ability to sympathize with our weaknesses. His triumph over temptation, coupled with His perfectly submitted life, enabled Him to carry out the redemptive plan of the cross.

Because of His victory, we can have confidence that when we face temptation, we have a High Priest who understands our struggles and was tempted as we are yet remained without sin. This gives us hope and reassurance in our own battles with temptation.

Why Does It Matter?

The Gospel in its entirety hinges on this essential truth: if Jesus were not sinless, there would be no sacrifice for sin. Without a perfect sacrifice, salvation would be impossible, leaving humanity utterly hopeless and eternally condemned. Paul beautifully and succinctly explains this in 2 Corinthians:

"For God made Christ, who never sinned, to be the offering for our sin, so that we could be made right with God through Christ."
2 Corinthians 5:21 NLT

Jesus was the perfect "offering" required for the atonement of sin, spotless and blameless, as described earlier. The ultimate purpose of this offering was clear: *"so that we could be made right with God through Christ."* Consider this profound truth: God Himself entered the world, first as a baby and then as a man, faced temptation in every way yet remained sinless, and finally subjected Himself to ridicule, torture, and death—all for the purpose of reconciling us to Himself.

Peter elaborates on this in his first epistle:

"For you know that God paid a ransom to save you from the empty life you inherited from your ancestors. And it was not paid with mere gold or silver, which lose their value. It was the precious blood of Christ, the sinless, spotless Lamb of God. God chose him as your ransom long before the world began, but now in these last days he has been revealed for your sake."
1 Peter 1:18-20 NLT

Our redemption is entirely dependent upon Christ's sinless life and His substitutionary death. Jesus was the only offering capable of fully satisfying God's righteous wrath against sin. His sacrifice accomplished what the Law could never achieve. Paul emphasizes this in his letter to the Romans:

"The law of Moses was unable to save us because of the weakness of our sinful nature. So God did what the law could not do. He sent his own Son in a body like the bodies we sinners have. And in that body God declared an end to sin's control over us by giving his Son as a sacrifice for our sins. He did this so that the just requirement of the law would be fully satisfied for us, who no longer follow our sinful nature but instead follow the Spirit."
Romans 8:3-4 NLT

In conclusion, the Bible unequivocally teaches that Jesus Christ was completely sinless. This means He perfectly conformed to the holy character and will of God in every way. He did not possess a sin nature, never committed a sinful act, and never harbored a wrong thought, attitude, or intent. Furthermore, He never failed to perform the good deeds that should have been done. This sinless perfection was essential for His role as Savior and the basis of our salvation, giving us hope and reconciliation with God through Him.

Further Study

1. What does Scripture teach about the sinlessness of Jesus? Consider passages such as Hebrews 4:15, 1 Peter 2:22, and 2 Corinthians 5:21.
2. Why is Jesus' sinlessness essential for His role as the perfect sacrifice for sin and our mediator before God?
3. How does Jesus' sinlessness set Him apart from all other humans, and what does this reveal about His divine and human natures?
4. What evidence from Jesus' life and ministry demonstrates His sinlessness in thought, word, and action?
5. How does Jesus' victory over temptation, such as His experience in the wilderness (Matthew 4:1-11), affirm His sinlessness?
6. What practical significance does Jesus' sinlessness have for Christians today, especially regarding our ability to trust Him as Savior and follow His example?

Additional Notes:

8. Substitutionary Atonement

Key Terms

1. **Substitutionary Atonement** - The doctrine that Jesus Christ died in the place of sinners, bearing the punishment they deserved so that they might be reconciled to God (Isaiah 53:4-6; 1 Peter 2:24).
2. **Propitiation** - The act of satisfying the wrath of God through Jesus' sacrificial death, which turned away divine judgment and restored favor to humanity (Romans 3:25; 1 John 2:2).
3. **Imputation** - The transfer of righteousness and guilt, where Jesus bore humanity's sin, and His righteousness is credited to believers through faith (2 Corinthians 5:21; Romans 4:5).
4. **Reconciliation** - The restoration of a broken relationship between God and humanity, made possible through Jesus' atoning death (Romans 5:10-11; Colossians 1:20).
5. **Sacrifice** - The offering of Jesus as the perfect Lamb of God, whose death fulfilled the Old Testament sacrificial system and removed sin once and for all (Hebrews 9:13-14; John 1:29).
6. **Ransom** - The price Jesus paid through His death to liberate sinners from slavery to sin and death (Mark 10:45; 1 Timothy 2:6).

What Is Substitutionary Atonement?

Substitutionary Atonement refers to the doctrine of our reconciliation with God through the sacrifice of Jesus Christ on the cross. Simply put, it means that Jesus died in the place of sinners, acting as our substitute, so that the death sentence we deserved could be nullified. This doctrine lies at the very heart of the Gospel, emphasizing the depth of God's love and the enormity of Christ's sacrifice on our behalf.

The Old Testament contains powerful prophecies that point to this substitutionary atonement and the coming Messiah who would suffer and die to bring forgiveness and restoration. One of the clearest examples is found in Isaiah 53:5:

"But he was pierced for our rebellion, crushed for our sins. He was beaten so we could be whole. He was whipped so we could be healed." Isaiah 53:5 NLT

This prophecy, written centuries before Christ's crucifixion, vividly describes the atonement and highlights the suffering Jesus endured for the sake of our salvation.

As we will explore further in future lessons, this doctrine also underscores our desperate need for faith and God's grace. It reminds us that salvation is not something we can earn through good works or personal merit but is instead a gift freely given by God. The Apostle Paul explains this truth in his letter to the Ephesians:

"God saved you by his grace when you believed. And you can't take credit for this; it is a gift from God. Salvation is not a reward for the good things we have done, so none of us can boast about it." Ephesians 2:8-9 NLT

Substitutionary Atonement reveals the profound depth of God's grace, the necessity of faith, and the sufficiency of Christ's sacrifice to restore us to a right relationship with God. It is through His work on the cross, not our own efforts, that we find true redemption and eternal hope.

What Did Jesus Have to Say About It?

It's important to realize that the writers of the Gospels did put the theology of atonement in Jesus' mouth. In fact, they honestly recorded their own lack of understanding about the necessity of His death. For example, Peter even rebuked Jesus when He foretold His suffering and death (Matthew 16:22). This transparency makes it clear that the disciples initially struggled to grasp the need for the Messiah to suffer in order to secure salvation. But was Jesus unclear about this? Absolutely not.

Christianity is an exclusive faith, centered on Jesus' atoning work—not in contradiction to His teachings, but because of them. As a rabbi, Jesus taught His disciples truths they had not perceived and could not fully understand at the time. It was only after His resurrection and the gift of the Holy Spirit that they came to comprehend the depth of His message and His work as the Good News—the news that Jesus came to die for the sins of the world.

Jesus Himself spoke directly about the purpose of His death, as recorded in the Gospel of John:

"I am the good shepherd. The good shepherd sacrifices his life for the sheep."
John 10:11 NLT

"Now my soul is deeply troubled. Should I pray, 'Father, save me from this hour'? But this is the very reason I came!"
John 12:27 NLT

In the Gospel of Mark, Jesus makes it clear that His death was meant to "ransom" many:

"For even the Son of Man came not to be served but to serve others and to give his life as a ransom for many."
Mark 10:45 NLT

These statements reveal that Jesus fully understood and embraced His mission to give His life for humanity. His death was not a tragic misunderstanding or a failure, but the fulfillment of His purpose as the Savior. Through His teachings, His disciples—and ultimately the world—would come to see His sacrifice as the cornerstone of salvation.

Why Was It Necessary?

In Lesson 5, we explored the concepts of "original sin" and "human depravity." Through Adam's failure in the Garden of Eden, sin entered the world, corrupting all of God's creation on Earth. This is evident in Genesis 3:17 and Romans 5:12:

"And to the man he said, 'Since you listened to your wife and ate from the tree whose fruit I commanded you not to eat, the ground is cursed because of you. All your life you will struggle to scratch a living from it.'"
Genesis 3:17 NLT

"When Adam sinned, sin entered the world. Adam's sin brought death, so death spread to everyone, for everyone sinned."
Romans 5:12 NLT

Because of sin, all humanity carries a "debt" that must be paid. Every human being is guilty of sin, as Paul makes clear in Romans 3:23:

"For everyone has sinned; we all fall short of God's glorious standard."
Romans 3:23, NLT

This debt of sin deserves punishment. Because God is holy and just, He cannot overlook sin or dismiss it without consequence. This reality is what led to the establishment of the sacrificial system in the Old Testament:

"For the life of the body is in its blood. I have given you the blood on the altar to purify you, making you right with the Lord. It is the blood, given in exchange for a life, that makes purification possible."
Leviticus 17:11 NLT

The writer of Hebrews confirms the necessity of this system and its reliance on the shedding of blood for forgiveness:

"In fact, according to the law of Moses, nearly everything was purified with blood. For without the shedding of blood, there is no forgiveness."
Hebrews 9:22 NLT

In the Old Testament, God instituted animal sacrifices as a means for sinners to receive forgiveness. By faith, those who identified with the sacrificed animal recognized its death as a substitute for their own punishment. However, this system was ultimately insufficient. It could not fully atone for humanity's sin nature or the imputed sin of Adam. The sacrifices were temporary and incomplete, pointing toward a greater solution.

Because of this, it was necessary for Jesus to willingly lay down His life as the ultimate and perfect sacrifice. His death fulfilled the requirements of the law and fully atoned for humanity's sin, offering complete redemption:

"But Christ has rescued us from the curse pronounced by the law. When he was hung on the cross, he took upon himself the curse for our wrongdoing. For it is written in the Scriptures, 'Cursed is everyone who is hung on a tree.'"
Galatians 3:13 NLT

Through Jesus' sacrificial death, the insufficiency of the Old Testament system was replaced by the sufficiency of Christ's finished work, offering forgiveness and salvation to all who believe in Him.

How Does It Work?

Jesus Christ is God and, as such, is an infinite being. (For more on this, see the lesson, "The Deity of Jesus.")

"In the beginning the Word already existed. The Word was with God, and the Word was God."
John 1:1 NLT

In contrast, we are finite, created beings. The sins we commit are against an infinite God, and therefore the punishment for those sins must also be infinite. This infinite punishment can be carried out in one of two ways: either an infinite being must die once to pay for all sins (the cross), or finite beings must endure eternal punishment (hell).

In His love, Jesus willingly offered Himself as the ultimate sacrifice, dying in our place on the cross. As an infinite being, His one-time payment for sin satisfied God's holy requirements completely and forever. The writer of Hebrews explains this beautifully:

"For God's will was for us to be made holy by the sacrifice of the body of Jesus Christ, once for all time. Under the old covenant, the priest stands and ministers before the altar day after day, offering the same sacrifices again and again, which can never take away sins. But our High Priest offered himself to God as a single sacrifice for sins, good for all time. Then he sat down in the place of honor at God's right hand. There he waits until his enemies are humbled and made a footstool under his feet. For by that one offering he forever made perfect those who are being made holy."
Hebrews 10:10-14 NLT

Through this act, God made Christ the offering for our sin so that we could be reconciled to Him:

"For God made Christ, who never sinned, to be the offering for our sin, so that we could be made right with God through Christ."
2 Corinthians 5:21 NLT

This atonement is further affirmed in 1 Peter 3:18, which emphasizes the completeness and sufficiency of Christ's sacrifice:

"Christ suffered for our sins once for all time. He never sinned, but he died for sinners to bring you safely home to God. He suffered physical death, but he was raised to life in the Spirit."
1 Peter 3:18 NLT

The infinite sacrifice of Jesus bridges the gap between a holy God and sinful humanity. His death and resurrection provide the only way for us to be made holy, forgiven, and reconciled to God for eternity.

What Does It Mean For Us?

According to Scripture, sin must be paid for, as clearly stated in Romans 6:23:

"For the wages of sin is death, but the free gift of God is eternal life through Christ Jesus our Lord."
Romans 6:23 NLT

This passage teaches us two crucial truths. First, it reminds us that without Christ's sacrifice and the doctrine of substitutionary atonement, humanity would be hopelessly doomed. In the Bible, "death" refers to separation. Physical death occurs when the soul is separated from the body. Spiritual death, however, occurs when a person is separated from God due to sin. For those who die without Jesus, this spiritual death results in eternal separation from God in hell, a fate from which there is no escape.

The second truth in this verse is the hope it offers: eternal life is available through Jesus Christ to all who believe. This eternal life was made possible through the shedding of Jesus' blood, which fulfilled the requirements of atonement and confirmed the significance of blood as a symbol of life, as seen earlier in Leviticus 17:11. The writer of Hebrews underscores the permanence and sufficiency of Jesus' sacrifice:

"With his own blood—not the blood of goats and calves—he entered the Most Holy Place once for all time and secured our redemption forever."
Hebrews 9:12 NLT

Tragically, many still reject this gift and will bear the consequences of their sin, paying the price themselves in hell for eternity. Yet, God, in His love and mercy, sent His Son, Jesus Christ, to pay for the sins of all who would believe. There is no more significant or urgent decision than accepting this gift of salvation. The time to repent of sin and place your trust in Jesus is now—while you are alive and the opportunity for atonement remains available.

The writer of Hebrews offers this sobering warning:

"Be careful then, dear brothers and sisters. Make sure that your own hearts are not evil and unbelieving, turning you away from the living God. You must warn each other every day, while it is still "today," so that none of you will be deceived by sin and hardened against God. For if we are faithful to the end, trusting God just as firmly as when we first believed, we will share in all that belongs to Christ. Remember what it says: "Today when you hear his voice, don't harden your hearts as Israel did when they rebelled.""
Hebrews 3:12-15 NLT

Eternal life is a gift freely offered, but it requires a response. Accepting Jesus' sacrifice through repentance and faith is the only way to escape the penalty of sin and share in the eternal joy that comes from being united with Christ.

Further Study

1. What is substitutionary atonement, and how is this concept explained in key Bible passages such as Isaiah 53:4-6, 1 Peter 2:24, and Romans 3:23-25?
2. Why was it necessary for Jesus to die as a substitute for sinners? How does this fulfill both God's justice and His mercy?
3. How does the Old Testament sacrificial system, particularly the concept of the sin offering (e.g., Leviticus 16), foreshadow Jesus' role as the ultimate substitute?
4. What does Jesus' cry, "It is finished" (John 19:30), reveal about the completion and sufficiency of His atoning work?
5. How does substitutionary atonement address the problem of human sin and provide a way for reconciliation with God?
6. What is the significance of 2 Corinthians 5:21 NLT, which states, "For God made Christ, who never sinned, to be the offering for our sin, so that we could be made right with God through Christ." in understanding the doctrine of substitutionary atonement?

Additional Notes:

9. The Necessity of God's Grace

Key Terms

1. **Grace** - The unmerited favor and kindness of God toward humanity, providing salvation and blessings that we do not deserve (Ephesians 2:8-9; Titus 2:11).
2. **Common Grace** - The grace of God that extends to all people, sustaining creation, restraining sin, and providing blessings like life, health, and provision (Matthew 5:45; Acts 14:17).
3. **Saving Grace** - The specific grace of God that brings sinners to salvation through faith in Jesus Christ, rescuing them from sin and eternal separation from God (Titus 3:4-7; Romans 5:20-21).
4. **Justification** - The act of God declaring a sinner righteous through faith in Jesus Christ, made possible by His grace (Romans 3:24; Galatians 2:16).
5. **Sanctification** - The process by which believers are made holy and conformed to the image of Christ, a work that begins with God's grace and continues through His Spirit (2 Thessalonians 2:13; Philippians 1:6).
6. **Mercy** - The compassion and forgiveness of God that spares sinners from the punishment they deserve, closely tied to His grace (Psalm 103:10-12; Hebrews 4:16).

Grace appears in Scripture over 150 times, emphasizing its central role in God's plan for salvation. One of my favorite examples is found in Ephesians 2:8-9, where the Apostle Paul, under the inspiration of the Holy Spirit, makes a profound statement: *"God saved you by his grace."*

"God saved you by his grace when you believed. And you can't take credit for this; it is a gift from God. Salvation is not a reward for the good things we have done, so none of us can boast about it."
Ephesians 2:8-9 NLT

Paul clearly states that salvation is entirely a work of grace—an undeserved gift from God—and not something we can earn or take credit for. This teaching was a significant departure from the prevailing Jewish cultural mindset of Paul's time. Many in first-century Judaism had distorted the truth, believing that salvation could be "earned" through strict adherence to the law, essentially implying that human works contributed to God's saving work. This concept also stood in stark contrast to Gentile cultures, which lacked a clear revelation of God and often relied on appeasing various deities through rituals and sacrifices.

Despite the clarity of this passage, many modern religious groups still hold to the belief that salvation results from a combination of faith, grace, and works. Among these are Catholic denominations, Mormons, and Jehovah's Witnesses. However, such a perspective fundamentally contradicts the biblical definition of grace. As Paul's teaching in Ephesians shows, grace ceases to be grace the moment it is earned or worked for. True grace is unmerited, entirely a gift from God, and the foundation of our salvation.

What is God's Grace?

When discussing grace, it's important to recognize the two types we encounter in life: *common grace* and *special grace*. Common grace is experienced by all people, regardless of their relationship with God. It reflects God's goodness evident in the beauty of nature, the joy of a delicious meal, or provision for everyone—including unbelievers and even those hostile toward Him. Common grace describes God's indiscriminate kindness and abundant blessings bestowed on all humanity through the daily gifts of earthly life. This grace is highlighted in the following passages:

"Don't you see how wonderfully kind, tolerant, and patient God is with you? Does this mean nothing to you? Can't you see that his kindness is intended to turn you from your sin?"
Romans 2:4 NLT

"In the past he permitted all the nations to go their own ways, but he never left them without evidence of himself and his goodness. For instance, he sends you rain and good crops and gives you food and joyful hearts."
Acts 14:16-17 NLT

In contrast, *special grace*—also referred to as *saving grace*—is uniquely given to those who accept Jesus Christ as their Lord and Savior. This is the grace Paul describes in Ephesians 2:8, which brings about salvation. Through this grace, we are forgiven, made righteous, and reconciled to God, not because of our works or worthiness, but solely through the work of Christ on the cross. It's a grace that we cannot earn, yet it is freely available to all who believe. Without this special grace, humanity remains hopeless, destined for eternal separation from God. Paul articulates this truth in Romans:

"For everyone has sinned; we all fall short of God's glorious standard. Yet God, in his grace, freely makes us right in his sight. He did this

through Christ Jesus when he freed us from the penalty for our sins."
Romans 3:23-24 NLT

Special grace is the divine intervention that transforms sinners into children of God. It reminds us that while we deserve judgment, we are offered forgiveness and eternal life through Christ—a gift that underscores the depth of God's love and mercy.

What Grace is Not.

We often encounter individuals who claim to be Christians yet live in ways that do not align with the example Jesus set for us. Frequently, they make statements defending sinful behavior, such as, *"I'm a forgiven child of God"* or *"God loves me even if I'm not perfect."* While these statements are not inherently untrue, they often reveal a misunderstanding of grace. Let me be clear: grace is not a license to sin. Paul addresses this directly in Romans 6:1:

"Well then, should we keep on sinning so that God can show us more and more of his wonderful grace?"
Romans 6:1 NLT

It's evident that even in Paul's time, believers struggled with the same flawed mindset: *"If God freely gives grace, then I can sin as much as I want."* This line of thinking fails to acknowledge the destructive nature of sin, disregards the call to live a Christlike life, and abuses the incredible gift of grace that God has given us.

Later in Romans 6, Paul elaborates on the implications of grace and the believer's relationship to sin:

"Sin is no longer your master, for you no longer live under the requirements of the law. Instead, you live under the freedom of God's grace. Well then, since God's grace has set us free from the law, does that mean we can go on sinning? Of course not! Don't you realize that you become the slave of whatever you choose to obey? You can be a

slave to sin, which leads to death, or you can choose to obey God, which leads to righteous living."
Romans 6:14-16 NLT

Paul's words remind us that grace doesn't liberate us to continue sinning; instead, it empowers us to live in righteousness. Sin no longer has mastery over us because of the transformative power of God's grace. Grace sets us free not to serve sin but to serve God.

As Charles Spurgeon profoundly put it:

"It is a test of our claim to be Christians. Does anger have dominion over you? Does murmuring and complaining? Does covetousness have dominion over you? Does pride? Does laziness have dominion over you? If sin has dominion over us, we should seriously ask if we are really converted."

If we continue to obey our sinful nature instead of living in obedience to God, who has set us free, we risk placing ourselves back under sin's authority. Grace is not a license to sin; rather, it is the power to live in freedom from sin's control. Persisting in sin draws us away from the grace of God and leads us back into spiritual bondage, undoing the freedom Christ has purchased for us.

Why Do We Need God's Grace?

Remember Lesson 5, the one on Human Depravity? We learned that since the Fall in the Garden of Eden, every human being has inherited a sin nature, and everyone sins. This sin separates us from God, brings physical and spiritual death, and sets us on a course toward eternal separation from Him—Hell. Without the grace of God, both common and special, there would be no goodness in our world. James reminds us of this truth:

"So don't be misled, my dear brothers and sisters. Whatever is good and perfect is a gift coming down to us from God our Father, who

created all the lights in the heavens. He never changes or casts a shifting shadow."
James 1:16-17 NLT

There is no goodness apart from the goodness of God. Anything good within us or through us comes only by His grace. God's grace saves us, justifies us, sanctifies us, and empowers us to serve Him. Without His grace, the world would descend into chaos—quite literally Hell on Earth—and we would be utterly lost. Thankfully, God's goodness and love extend beyond what we deserve. Even though humanity chose the path of destruction, God graciously intervened. Jesus explained this in the Gospel of John:

"For this is how God loved the world: He gave his one and only Son, so that everyone who believes in him will not perish but have eternal life. God sent his Son into the world not to judge the world, but to save the world through him."
John 3:16-17 NLT

We were destined for Hell, but God made a way where there was no way. God does not wish for anyone to be lost; instead, He desires that "none shall perish" and extends His grace to all who will accept it. The Apostle Paul further reveals that this was not an afterthought—God's plan of grace through Christ was set in motion *"before the beginning of time."*

"For God saved us and called us to live a holy life. He did this, not because we deserved it, but because that was his plan from before the beginning of time—to show us his grace through Christ Jesus."
2 Timothy 1:9 NLT

So why do we need God's grace? It is the channel through which we receive every good and perfect gift from Him, most importantly, salvation. Without grace, we have no hope, but through grace, we are given life, purpose, and the opportunity to be reconciled to our Creator.

What is Grace's Greatest Enemy?

I believe pride is the greatest enemy of God's grace. It manifests in many forms, often appearing innocent, such as independence and self-reliance. Pride can quietly take root deep within our souls, subtly plotting its rebellion against God. It elevates us above others and ultimately tempts us to take God's rightful place in our lives.

Pride deceives us into believing that we can duplicate the work of the cross, often through our own efforts or "good works." It convinces us that we can be "good enough" on our own and therefore have no need for God's grace. This self-deception leads to prayerlessness, ingratitude, hypocrisy, and every kind of evil. Over time, pride hardens the heart, causing us to reject God's grace entirely, leaving the proud to bear the weight of their own sins.

Scripture warns us about the consequences of pride:
"And he gives grace generously. As the Scriptures say, 'God opposes the proud but gives grace to the humble.'"
James 4:6 NLT

Pride ultimately puts us in direct opposition to God and separates us from the grace that He freely offers to the humble. Acknowledging our dependence on God and surrendering our pride is essential to receiving His transformative grace.

What Does Grace Mean for Us?

Because of the grace of God, we receive something we could never earn or deserve. Salvation is the most obvious and significant result of this grace, but God's grace encompasses so much more—it provides everything we need to live a Christ-like life. In Ephesians 2:8-10, we see not only the gift of grace but also its purpose and calling:

"God saved you by his grace when you believed. And you can't take credit for this; it is a gift from God. Salvation is not a reward for the good things we have done, so none of us can boast about it. For we are God's masterpiece. He has created us anew in Christ Jesus, so we can do the good things he planned for us long ago."
Ephesians 2:8-10 NLT

Through God's grace, He reveals Himself to us (*Revealed Theology*), drawing us into a relationship with Him (*Saving Grace*). This grace is not merely about escaping judgment—it's far more than "fire insurance." It is part of a greater call: to live for His honor and glory. We fulfill this call, in part, by doing the "good things He planned for us long ago." God's grace not only saves us but also prepares and equips us for the work He has called us to accomplish. Paul elaborates on this in Romans 12:6-8, showing how God's grace enables us to serve Him through the gifts He bestows:

"In his grace, God has given us different gifts for doing certain things well. So if God has given you the ability to prophesy, speak out with as much faith as God has given you. If your gift is serving others, serve them well. If you are a teacher, teach well. If your gift is to encourage others, be encouraging. If it is giving, give generously. If God has given you leadership ability, take the responsibility seriously. And if you have a gift for showing kindness to others, do it gladly."
Romans 12:6-8 NLT

God's grace is indispensable. It is through His grace that we come to know Him, receive salvation, and are empowered to serve Him faithfully. Without God's grace, there would be no goodness in the world, no hope for redemption, and no ability to carry out the good works He has prepared for us. His grace is the foundation for our relationship with Him, our calling, and our purpose.

Further Study

1. What is grace, and how does the Bible define and describe it? Consider passages such as Ephesians 2:8-9, Titus 2:11, and Romans 3:23-24.
2. Why is God's grace necessary for salvation, and what role does human effort or works play in light of this necessity?
3. How does the doctrine of grace highlight humanity's inability to save itself and the depth of God's love and mercy?
4. In what ways does God's grace sustain believers not only for salvation but also for daily living and spiritual growth? Reflect on 2 Corinthians 12:9 and Hebrews 4:16.
5. What is the relationship between God's grace and faith? How does Ephesians 2:8-9 illustrate this connection?
6. How should the reality of God's grace affect the way Christians view themselves, others, and their relationship with God?

Additional Notes:

10. The Necessity of Faith

Key Terms

1. **Faith** - Complete trust and confidence in God, believing His promises and acting on His Word, even when unseen or uncertain (Hebrews 11:1; Romans 10:17).
2. **Saving Faith** - The trust in Jesus Christ as Lord and Savior, leading to salvation through His finished work on the cross (Ephesians 2:8-9; John 3:16).
3. **Justification** - The act of God declaring a sinner righteous by grace through faith in Jesus Christ (Romans 5:1; Galatians 2:16).
4. **Perseverance** - The continuing trust in God and adherence to faith in the face of trials, sustained by His grace (James 1:2-4; Philippians 1:6).
5. **Works** - Actions that flow from genuine faith, demonstrating its reality and alignment with God's will, but not as a basis for salvation (James 2:17-18; Ephesians 2:10).
6. **Trust** - A central component of faith, involving reliance on God's character, promises, and faithfulness in all circumstances (Proverbs 3:5-6; Psalm 9:10).

Faith lies at the very heart of Christianity and the Christian life. It is how we receive salvation and the essential ingredient that enables us to please God and fulfill His purpose for our lives. Yet, faith can often feel elusive or difficult to grasp. To make matters even more challenging, Jesus describes faith in a way that almost seems mystical, as if it belongs in a lesson from Master Yoda on the planet Dagobah:

""You don't have enough faith," Jesus told them. "I tell you the truth, if you had faith even as small as a mustard seed, you could say to this mountain, 'Move from here to there,' and it would move. Nothing would be impossible.""
Matthew 17:20 NLT

This powerful statement leaves us asking: What is faith, really? Why is it so essential to our relationship with God and our role in His plan? Understanding the true nature of faith helps us grasp why it is central to living a life that honors God and relies on His promises.

What is Faith?

Faith is one of those words that often feels shrouded in mystery. We know we are supposed to have it, even if we don't fully understand what it is. Many hesitate to ask for clarification, fearing they might discover they lack it—or worse, that others might realize it too. Part of the confusion surrounding faith arises from the varying definitions and uses we encounter in daily life. Genuine faith, however, involves abandoning all reliance on human effort and placing total dependence on God's character, actions, and promises as revealed in His Word.

Perhaps the closest the Bible comes to providing a precise definition of faith is found in Hebrews 11:1, where the writer of Hebrews eloquently explains:

"Faith shows the reality of what we hope for; it is the evidence of things we cannot see."
Hebrews 11:1 NLT

"Now faith is the assurance (title deed, confirmation) of things hoped for (divinely guaranteed), and the evidence of things not seen [the conviction of their reality—faith comprehends as fact what cannot be experienced by the physical senses]."
Hebrews 11:1 AMP

But what does this mean in practical terms? From this passage, we can see that faith is confident trust—confidence that God is who He says He is and trust that He can and will do what He says He can do. Faith is not a blind leap; it is rooted in God's reliability and His proven character throughout Scripture.

It's also important to understand that faith goes beyond what our senses can perceive. While it has "reasons," those reasons must be discerned spiritually. Just as our physical senses allow us to perceive the natural world, faith is the spiritual faculty through which we perceive and comprehend the things of God. Faith bridges the gap between the seen and the unseen, enabling us to trust in divine realities even when they are beyond physical evidence.

What Faith is Not.

Faith is not blind. One of the most damaging definitions of faith describes it as "belief in something despite lacking any evidence for it." This concept of blind faith fosters a "sit down and shut up" kind of atmosphere, where questions are discouraged, and doubt is seen as a lack of commitment. Such an environment alienates people and often leads to them leaving the Church. However, God does not ask us to have blind faith. On the contrary, He invites us to have faith based on the evidence He has provided. For those of us alive today, our faith is grounded in the revelation of God—His character, His power, and His ability. We see evidence of His love and grace, as discussed in the previous chapter. This evidence is the foundation on which we are called to respond in faith.

Faith is not works. Sometimes, even with good intentions, people misunderstand faith and present it as though it were a "work." This misunderstanding can lead to a transactional view of salvation: God offers grace, we offer faith, and the result is salvation. But this is not what Scripture teaches. Faith is not something we produce on our own or offer to God in exchange for His grace. Rather, faith itself is a gift from God, a result of His grace working in us. Apart from Him, we could neither possess faith nor respond to Him in belief. This understanding keeps us grounded in the truth that salvation is entirely a work of God's grace, not something we can achieve or earn.

Why Is Faith Important?

The great preacher Dwight L. Moody often spoke of three kinds of faith in Jesus Christ: struggling faith, like a person floundering and fearful in deep water; clinging faith, like someone hanging onto the side of a boat; and resting faith, where the person is safe inside the boat, secure and strong enough to extend a hand to help others.

When we consider the importance of faith, it's crucial to not only reflect on where we currently stand but also to examine how faith impacts three key areas: our relationship with God, our interactions with Him, and the way we engage with the world around us. Let's begin with a foundational passage from Hebrews:

"And it is impossible to please God without faith. Anyone who wants to come to him must believe that God exists and that he rewards those who sincerely seek him."
Hebrews 11:6 NLT

The writer of Hebrews makes an astonishing statement: without faith, it is impossible to please God. No amount of prayer, good works, or church attendance is acceptable to Him if it is done without faith. Faith is essential to approach God and experience a personal relationship with Him. Thankfully, faith is a gift of grace available to all. Just as salvation is available to everyone, so too is the faith necessary to please God. This passage underscores the fundamental importance of faith.

Saving Faith

The most obvious aspect of faith is saving faith, which makes us right before God and brings about salvation. Many theologians teach that saving faith consists of three essential elements: understanding, acceptance, and trust. Without all three, a person cannot have saving faith. It is not enough to merely believe in God's existence—*even the demons believe that much* (James 2:19). Saving faith requires confident trust in God and His promises.

Paul explains this in Romans, showing how the Gospel, God's grace, and our faith work together to bring salvation:

"For I am not ashamed of this Good News about Christ. It is the power of God at work, saving everyone who believes—the Jew first and also the Gentile. This Good News tells us how God makes us right in his sight. This is accomplished from start to finish by faith. As the Scriptures say, 'It is through faith that a righteous person has life.'"
Romans 1:16-17 NLT

Saving faith is always accompanied by repentance. Repentance and faith are two sides of the same coin—it is impossible to truly place your faith in Jesus Christ as Savior without first changing your mind about your sin, who Jesus is, and what He has done.

"Repent of your sins and turn to God, for the Kingdom of Heaven is near."
Matthew 3:2, NLT

Faith in Our Interactions with God

Faith also directly impacts how we interact with God. In Matthew 9, we see that the faith of the paralyzed man and his friends prompted Jesus to respond:

116

"Some people brought to him a paralyzed man on a mat. Seeing their faith, Jesus said to the paralyzed man, 'Be encouraged, my child! Your sins are forgiven.'"
Matthew 9:2 NLT

Conversely, a lack of faith can hinder our interactions with God. In Matthew 13, Jesus faced unbelief in His hometown, which limited His ministry there:

"And they were deeply offended and refused to believe in him. Then Jesus told them, 'A prophet is honored everywhere except in his own hometown and among his own family.' And so he did only a few miracles there because of their unbelief."
Matthew 13:57-58 NLT

Jesus also recognizes the degree of faith people exhibit. In Matthew 14, He gently rebukes Peter for his weak faith when Peter begins to sink while walking on water:

"Jesus immediately reached out and grabbed him. 'You have so little faith,' Jesus said. 'Why did you doubt me?'"
Matthew 14:31 NLT

In contrast, in Matthew 15, Jesus commends a woman for her great faith before healing her daughter:

"Dear woman," Jesus said to her, "your faith is great. Your request is granted." And her daughter was instantly healed.
Matthew 15:28 NLT

Faith is a crucial element in how we experience God's presence and power. While God is sovereign and not limited by human faith, Scripture demonstrates that He notices our faith and often moves, speaks, and acts in response to it.

Faith in the World Around Us

Faith should also shape how we interact with the world. True saving faith, which results in salvation, is a gift of grace. As we learned in the previous chapter, salvation cannot be earned—it is by faith and grace alone. However, true biblical faith will always express itself through works. Our actions should be evidence of the inward change that faith has brought about.

Paul writes in Romans:

"He will judge everyone according to what they have done. He will give eternal life to those who keep on doing good, seeking after the glory and honor and immortality that God offers."
Romans 2:6-7 NLT

Conversely, Paul warns that those who live in sin will not inherit the Kingdom of God:

"Don't you realize that those who do wrong will not inherit the Kingdom of God? Don't fool yourselves. Those who indulge in sexual sin, or who worship idols, or commit adultery, or are male prostitutes, or practice homosexuality, or are thieves, or greedy people, or drunkards, or are abusive, or cheat people—none of these will inherit the Kingdom of God."
(1 Corinthians 6:9-10, NLT)

James, the half-brother of Jesus, emphasizes the necessity of works as evidence of genuine faith:

"What good is it, dear brothers and sisters, if you say you have faith but don't show it by your actions? Can that kind of faith save anyone? Suppose you see a brother or sister who has no food or clothing, and you say, 'Good-bye and have a good day; stay warm and eat well'—but then you don't give that person any food or clothing. What good does that do? So you see, faith by itself isn't enough. Unless it produces good

deeds, it is dead and useless."
James 2:14-17 NLT

Faith is not meant to be passive or neutral in our lives. It is a gift of God's grace, necessary for salvation, and designed to transform how we interact with Him and the world. Genuine faith produces visible results, shaping our actions, attitudes, and relationships as we live in obedience to God and reflect His love to others.

How Do You Get More Faith?

If faith is as vital as Scripture teaches, then increasing its presence in our lives should be a priority. Dwight L. Moody once shared this insightful perspective on faith:

"I prayed for faith and thought it would strike me like lightning. But faith did not come. One day I read, 'Now faith comes by hearing, and hearing by the Word of God.' I had closed my Bible and prayed for faith. I now began to study my Bible, and faith has been growing ever since."

Moody's conclusion aligns perfectly with what Paul wrote in Romans 10:

"So faith comes from hearing, that is, hearing the Good News about Christ."
Romans 10:17 NLT

As we considered earlier in this chapter, genuine faith involves abandoning all reliance on self-efforts and placing complete trust in God's character, actions, and promises. But where do we come to know God's character? Where can we see His actions and watch His promises unfold? The answer is simple: the Bible.

Scripture is where God has revealed Himself to us. Through it, we witness His faithfulness, power, and love displayed throughout history. Spending time in God's Word is not merely an academic exercise—it is essential for deepening our relationship with Him and allowing our faith to grow. As Moody experienced, immersing ourselves in the Word of God enables us to better understand who God is and strengthens the foundation of our trust in Him.

Further Study

1. What does the Bible teach about the importance of faith for salvation? Consider passages like Hebrews 11:6, Romans 3:22, and Ephesians 2:8-9.
2. How is faith defined in Hebrews 11:1, and what does this definition reveal about its role in the believer's life?
3. Why is faith necessary to have a relationship with God, and how does it differ from relying on works or personal merit?
4. What is the connection between faith and obedience? How does genuine faith produce actions that align with God's will? (See James 2:17-18.)
5. How does Jesus' teaching in John 3:16 demonstrate the centrality of faith in God's plan for salvation?
6. In what ways does faith sustain believers during trials and challenges? How can passages like 2 Corinthians 5:7 and Proverbs 3:5-6 encourage Christians to walk by faith?

Additional Notes:

11. Jesus' Bodily Resurrection

Key Terms

1. **Resurrection** - The act of Jesus rising from the dead on the third day after His crucifixion, demonstrating His victory over sin, death, and the grave (Luke 24:6-7; 1 Corinthians 15:3-4).
2. **First Fruits** - A term used to describe Jesus' resurrection as the first and guarantee of the future resurrection of all believers (1 Corinthians 15:20-23).
3. **Empty Tomb** - The physical evidence of Jesus' resurrection, where His body was no longer found, confirming His triumph over death (Matthew 28:5-6; John 20:1-9).
4. **Witnesses** - Individuals who encountered the risen Jesus and testified to His resurrection, including Mary Magdalene, the disciples, and over 500 others (1 Corinthians 15:5-8; John 20:11-29).
5. **Vindication** - The affirmation of Jesus' identity as the Son of God and His authority through His resurrection, proving His teachings and sacrifice were divinely approved (Romans 1:4; Acts 2:24).
6. **Hope** - The confident expectation of eternal life and victory over death for believers, made possible by Jesus' resurrection (1 Peter 1:3; Romans 6:5).

The bodily resurrection of Jesus is arguably the most significant aspect of the salvation narrative and the single greatest event in human history since creation. Every element of the Christian faith hinges on this truth. If Jesus had simply died without rising again, Christianity as we know it would not exist today. The resurrection is the ultimate confirmation of Jesus' identity as the Son of God, the fulfillment of prophecy, and the foundation of our hope for eternal life.

John MacArthur highlights the importance of this event:

"The resurrection of Jesus Christ is the single greatest event in the history of the world. It is so foundational to Christianity that no one who denies it can be a true Christian... A person who believes in a Christ who was not raised believes in a powerless Christ, a dead Christ. If Christ did not rise from the dead, then no redemption was accomplished at the cross and 'your faith is worthless,' Paul goes on to say; 'you are still in your sins' (v. 17). If Christ was not raised, His death was in vain, your faith in Him would be pointless, and your sins would still be counted against you with no hope of spiritual life."

Paul underscores this critical truth in his letter to the Corinthians:

"And if there is no resurrection of the dead, then Christ has not been raised. And if Christ has not been raised, then your faith is useless and you are still guilty of your sins. In that case, all who have died believing in Christ are lost!"
1 Corinthians 15:16-18 NLT

The resurrection is not merely a theological detail—it is the linchpin of the Gospel. Without it, the cross loses its power, and humanity remains trapped in sin with no hope of redemption. Through the resurrection, Jesus demonstrated His victory over sin, death, and the grave, securing eternal life for all who place their faith in Him. It is the ultimate assurance of God's redemptive plan and the cornerstone of the Christian faith.

What Do We Mean "Resurrection"?

Anastasis is the Greek word for resurrection. According to Strong's Concordance, *anastasis* means "a standing up, i.e., a resurrection, a raising up, rising." When we refer to the resurrection of Jesus, we mean quite literally that He was dead and then brought back to life. This was not merely a spiritual resurrection, but a physical one, as Jesus' body was raised from the dead. While this event is entirely outside the natural order and impossible to explain in modern terms, it demonstrates God's sovereignty as the author of life. God, who holds power over life and death, exercised His divine authority in raising Jesus from the grave. Despite what many—including myself—consider to be overwhelming evidence, there are those who claim the resurrection did not take place.

Various theories have been proposed to explain away the resurrection:

- **The Swoon Theory** suggests that Jesus didn't actually die but fell into a deep coma from the trauma of the Crucifixion. In this state, He supposedly "revived" in the cool atmosphere of the tomb, freed Himself from the tightly wrapped burial cloths, and then appeared to His disciples.
- **The No Burial Theory** claims that Jesus was never placed in a tomb but was instead thrown into a mass grave for criminals, as was customary for many Roman executions.
- **The Mass Hallucination Theory** posits that all those who claimed to have seen the risen Jesus were experiencing hallucinations driven by their intense desire to see Him alive again.
- **The Stolen Body Theory** suggests that Jesus' disciples stole His body to fabricate the fulfillment of His resurrection prophecy. This story is recorded in Scripture as having originated on the day the guards at Jesus' tomb reported to the chief priests what had occurred. The priests bribed the guards, instructing them to spread the false narrative that the disciples had stolen Jesus' body (Matthew 28:11–15).

It's crucial to emphasize that when we speak of Jesus' resurrection, we mean that He was physically dead and then raised to life again. Each of these alternative theories has been carefully examined over time and has a conclusive rebuttal. The resurrection of Jesus remains the cornerstone of the Christian faith, demonstrating God's power, fulfilling prophecy, and securing eternal life for those who believe.

What Does Old Testament Prophecy Say About It?

Old Testament prophecy can often seem ambiguous at first glance. This is especially true when it comes to the resurrection of the Messiah. However, with closer examination, it becomes clear that God's plan for the Messiah's resurrection was in place long before the birth of Jesus. The prophet Isaiah had much to say about the Savior, particularly in the "Suffering Servant" passage of Isaiah 53. In this remarkable prophecy, Isaiah writes:

"He had done no wrong and had never deceived anyone. But he was buried like a criminal; he was put in a rich man's grave. But it was the Lord's good plan to crush him and cause him grief. Yet when his life is made an offering for sin, he will have many descendants. He will enjoy a long life, and the Lord's good plan will prosper in his hands. When he sees all that is accomplished by his anguish, he will be satisfied. And because of his experience, my righteous servant will make it possible for many to be counted righteous, for he will bear all their sins." Isaiah 53:9-11, NLT

After describing the servant's death, Isaiah declares that *"He will enjoy a long life."* This statement points directly to resurrection since it is only through being raised from the dead that one can enjoy life after dying. A similar theme appears in Psalm 16, where David writes:

"For you will not leave my soul among the dead or allow your holy one to rot in the grave. You will show me the way of life, granting me the

joy of your presence and the pleasures of living with you forever."
Psalm 16:10-11 NLT

The Apostle Peter provides further clarity on this psalm during his sermon at Pentecost:

"Dear brothers, think about this! You can be sure that the patriarch David wasn't referring to himself, for he died and was buried, and his tomb is still here among us. But he was a prophet, and he knew God had promised with an oath that one of David's own descendants would sit on his throne. David was looking into the future and speaking of the Messiah's resurrection. He was saying that God would not leave him among the dead or allow his body to rot in the grave."
Acts 2:29-31 NLT

Other Old Testament passages also reference the resurrection of the Messiah, though many may initially seem cryptic. When studied carefully, these prophecies collectively reveal God's redemptive plan. Yet, perhaps the most powerful prophecy concerning the Messiah's death and resurrection came from Jesus Himself. As many have pointed out, if a man predicts His own death and resurrection and then fulfills it, we should take notice.

What Did Jesus Have To Say About It?

Jesus repeatedly predicted His death and resurrection, emphasizing that His rising from the dead was central to His message and ministry. This defining event was the cornerstone of His purpose and the ultimate proof of His identity. Years before His resurrection, Jesus made this statement while speaking to Jewish religious leaders. John's comment in verse 22 highlights how the disciples later recalled this moment and fully believed in both the Scriptures and Jesus' words:

"But the Jewish leaders demanded, 'What are you doing? If God gave you authority to do this, show us a miraculous sign to prove it.' 'All right,' Jesus replied. 'Destroy this temple, and in three days I will raise

it up.' 'What!' they exclaimed. 'It has taken forty-six years to build this Temple, and you can rebuild it in three days?' But when Jesus said 'this temple,' he meant his own body. After he was raised from the dead, his disciples remembered he had said this, and they believed both the Scriptures and what Jesus had said."
John 2:18-22 NLT

Jesus explicitly stated that His resurrection would serve as the ultimate sign of His divine authority and identity. In Matthew's Gospel, He refers to the "sign of Jonah" as an indication of His death and resurrection:

"But Jesus replied, 'Only an evil, adulterous generation would demand a miraculous sign; but the only sign I will give them is the sign of the prophet Jonah. For as Jonah was in the belly of the great fish for three days and three nights, so will the Son of Man be in the heart of the earth for three days and three nights.'"
Matthew 12:39-40 NLT

In the final months of His ministry, Jesus began to focus more explicitly on His impending crucifixion, death, and resurrection. He spoke plainly to His disciples, preparing them for what was to come and reaffirming the significance of these events:

"From then on Jesus began to tell his disciples plainly that it was necessary for him to go to Jerusalem, and that he would suffer many terrible things at the hands of the elders, the leading priests, and the teachers of religious law. He would be killed, but on the third day he would be raised from the dead."
Matthew 16:21 NLT

Notably, Jesus didn't just predict His resurrection—He claimed that He had the authority and power to raise Himself. While anyone can choose to lay down their life, only Jesus could take it up again, a testament to both His resurrection and His divine nature:

"The Father loves me because I sacrifice my life so I may take it back again. No one can take my life from me. I sacrifice it voluntarily. For I have the authority to lay it down when I want to and also to take it up again. For this is what my Father has commanded."
John 10:17-18, NLT

These declarations point to the unmatched authority and divinity of Jesus, underscoring the centrality of His resurrection in His mission and identity. The resurrection not only validated His claims but also became the defining event that secured hope and salvation for humanity.

What Did the Early Church Believe?

Jesus' predictions about His resurrection were not only frequent but widely known, even among His enemies. This is evident in the actions of the leading priests and Pharisees, who went to Pilate after His death to request that the tomb be sealed. Their concern over the disciples staging a fake resurrection highlights their awareness of Jesus' claims and creates significant challenges for alternate theories regarding the resurrection, such as the swoon theory, the stolen body theory, and the no burial theory.

"The next day, on the Sabbath, the leading priests and Pharisees went to see Pilate. They told him, 'Sir, we remember what that deceiver once said while he was still alive: "After three days I will rise from the dead." So we request that you seal the tomb until the third day. This will prevent his disciples from coming and stealing his body and then telling everyone he was raised from the dead! If that happens, we'll be worse off than we were at first.' Pilate replied, 'Take guards and secure it the best you can.' So they sealed the tomb and posted guards to protect it."
Matthew 27:62-66 NLT

Despite their planning and precautions, Jesus rose from the dead and left the sealed tomb. Interestingly, the religious leaders anticipated that the disciples might attempt to stage a resurrection, but they failed to understand Jesus' own words. In reality, the disciples were frightened and in hiding, with no plans to recover His body or proclaim a resurrection. There was no countdown or celebration awaiting Jesus' return. Instead, the first to encounter the risen Christ were several women who came to anoint His body, only to find an empty tomb.

"When they entered the tomb, they saw a young man clothed in a white robe sitting on the right side. The women were shocked, but the angel said, 'Don't be alarmed. You are looking for Jesus of Nazareth, who was crucified. He isn't here! He is risen from the dead! Look, this is where they laid his body. Now go and tell his disciples, including Peter, that Jesus is going ahead of you to Galilee. You will see him there, just as he told you before he died.'"
Mark 16:5-7 NLT

These women became the first to proclaim the Good News of the resurrection. Later that same day, Jesus appeared to two followers on the road to Emmaus and, that evening, to His disciples as they gathered behind locked doors. Eight days later, Jesus appeared again, this time allowing Thomas, who had been absent before, to touch His wounds. In awe, Thomas declared, *"My Lord and my God!"*

The resurrection was not a one-time event but a reality Jesus demonstrated repeatedly. In the opening of Acts, Luke confirms that Jesus appeared to His followers numerous times over 40 days, providing undeniable proof of His resurrection and teaching about the Kingdom of God:

"During the forty days after he suffered and died, he appeared to the apostles from time to time, and he proved to them in many ways that he was actually alive. And he talked to them about the Kingdom of God."
Acts 1:3 NLT

Paul also records that Jesus appeared to over 500 followers at once. This extraordinary claim is significant not only because of the sheer number of witnesses but because Paul essentially challenges his readers to verify the account, noting that many of those witnesses were still alive at the time. Paul himself encountered the risen Christ on the road to Damascus.

"After that, he was seen by more than 500 of his followers at one time, most of whom are still alive, though some have died."
1 Corinthians 15:6 NLT

"Last of all, as though I had been born at the wrong time, I also saw him."
1 Corinthians 15:8 NLT

The apostles' unwavering belief in the resurrection was so strong that most of them died as martyrs for their faith. John was the only apostle to avoid martyrdom, although tradition holds that he survived being boiled in oil before being exiled to Patmos. Early church history and tradition provide accounts of the other apostles' deaths:

- **James** was the first apostle martyred, as recorded in Acts 12:2.
- **Peter** was scourged and crucified. Tradition says he was crucified upside down at his request.
- **Andrew** was martyred in Patrae, Achaia.
- **Philip** was martyred in Heliopolis.
- **Bartholomew** was placed in a sack and thrown into the sea.
- **Thomas** was pierced with a lance in India.
- **Matthew** was killed in Ethiopia.
- **James (son of Alphaeus)** was stoned and beaten to death with a club.
- **Thaddaeus (Judas, son of James)** was either crucified or shot with arrows, according to different traditions.

- **Simon the Zealot** was crucified in Britain after preaching the gospel there.

These accounts highlight the unwavering faith of the apostles and the transformative power of the resurrection. Their willingness to face persecution and death is a compelling testament to the truth of their witness to the risen Christ.

Why Does It Matter?

American pastor, theologian, and apologist Tim Keller said, *"If Jesus rose from the dead, then you have to accept all that he said; if he didn't rise from the dead, then why worry about any of what he said? The issue on which everything hangs is not whether or not you like his teaching but whether or not he rose from the dead."*

This is a profound and absolutely true statement. When examining the life of Jesus, the resurrection becomes both the starting point for many and the culmination of faith. We know of Jesus today because of His resurrection, and we follow Him when we choose to believe it. The truth of the resurrection validates not only the testimony of Jesus but also the testimony of His disciples. Furthermore, it affirms the reliability and divine inspiration of the Scriptures as we read them today.

The resurrection not only validates Jesus' words but also confirms His sinless character and divine nature. If Jesus had lied about His identity or mission, He would not have been sinless, nor could He have been the Savior. As stated in John 10, Jesus claimed the power to raise Himself from the dead, a power reserved exclusively for God. This claim, fulfilled through the resurrection, stands as undeniable evidence of Jesus' deity and a profound demonstration of the immense power of God.

Moreover, the resurrection is a validation of God's existence and sovereignty. If God exists and is the Creator of the universe, He holds power over all creation, including life and death. His ability to raise the dead affirms His worthiness of our faith and worship. Conversely, a god who lacks such power would not be worthy of our trust or devotion. The resurrection, therefore, is not only the cornerstone of the Christian faith but also the ultimate proof of God's authority and the divine identity of Jesus Christ.

What Does It Mean For Us?

Only the Creator of life has the power to resurrect it after death. Even with all of today's medical advancements, the best humanity can achieve in its own power is resuscitation. The ability to create life, to restore it from death, belongs solely to God. Only He can remove the sting of death and bring true victory over the grave.

"Then, when our dying bodies have been transformed into bodies that will never die, this Scripture will be fulfilled: 'Death is swallowed up in victory. O death, where is your victory? O death, where is your sting?'"
1 Corinthians 15:54-55 NLT

Because Jesus was the first to be raised to eternal life, as believers, we can also look forward to our resurrection. His triumph over death ensures that we no longer have to live in fear of death or face a hopeless and bleak future. Through His resurrection, Jesus has secured eternal life for all who believe in Him. This means we can look forward to spending eternity with our risen Savior, experiencing the fullness of life after this life.

"Jesus told her, 'I am the resurrection and the life. Anyone who believes in me will live, even after dying. Everyone who lives in me and believes in me will never ever die. Do you believe this, Martha?'"
John 11:25-26 NLT

To close this chapter, I want to share a powerful quote from Athanasius, the same Athanasius whose creed we studied in Chapter 3 while learning about the Trinity. His words encapsulate the hope and assurance we have in Christ's resurrection.

"He, the Life of all, our Lord and Saviour, did not arrange the manner of his own death lest He should seem to be afraid of some other kind. No. He accepted and bore upon the cross a death inflicted by others, and those other His special enemies, a death which to them was supremely terrible and by no means to be faced; and He did this in order that, by destroying even this death, He might Himself be believed to be the Life, and the power of death be recognised as finally annulled. A marvellous and mighty paradox has thus occurred, for the death which they thought to inflict on Him as dishonour and disgrace has become the glorious monument to death's defeat." - Athanasius of Alexandria

Further Study

1. What biblical evidence supports the bodily resurrection of Jesus? Consider key passages such as Luke 24:36-43, 1 Corinthians 15:3-8, and John 20:24-29.
2. Why is the bodily resurrection of Jesus essential to the Christian faith? How does Paul explain its importance in 1 Corinthians 15:12-19?
3. What does Jesus' bodily resurrection reveal about His victory over sin, death, and the grave? How does this victory provide hope for believers?
4. How did Jesus' bodily resurrection fulfill Old Testament prophecies and His own predictions during His ministry? (See Psalm 16:10, Isaiah 53:10-12, and Matthew 16:21.)
5. What role did the eyewitness accounts of Jesus' resurrection play in establishing the credibility of this event in the early Church?
6. How does the bodily resurrection of Jesus impact the Christian hope for eternal life and the promise of our future resurrection? (See Romans 8:11 and Philippians 3:20-21.)

Additional Notes:

12. Jesus' Bodily Ascension

Key Terms

1. **Ascension** - The event where Jesus physically rose into heaven in the presence of His disciples, marking the end of His earthly ministry and His return to the Father (Acts 1:9-11; Luke 24:50-51).
2. **Intercession** - Jesus' ongoing role at the right hand of God, where He advocates and mediates on behalf of believers (Hebrews 7:25; Romans 8:34).
3. **Exaltation** - The glorification of Jesus following His ascension, affirming His divine authority and position as King and Lord (Philippians 2:9-11; Ephesians 1:20-23).
4. **Session** - A theological term describing Jesus sitting at the right hand of the Father, signifying His completed work of redemption and His reign over all creation (Mark 16:19; Hebrews 1:3).
5. **Promise** - The assurance Jesus gave to send the Holy Spirit to empower His followers after His ascension (John 16:7; Acts 1:4-5).
6. **Return** - The future event when Jesus will come again in glory, as foretold by the angels at His ascension (Acts 1:11; Revelation 22:12).

The bodily ascension of Jesus is inseparably connected to His bodily resurrection. While they are distinct events, each marking the completion of a unique aspect of His redemptive work, one cannot exist without the other. If there were no resurrection, Jesus could not have ascended; if He did not ascend, we are left with the question: where is His body? The resurrection confirms His victory over sin and death, while the ascension affirms His glorification and return to the Father, completing His earthly mission.

The theologian Justus Knecht provides an excellent summary of the significance of the ascension in his commentary. He captures the profound meaning of this pivotal event in Christ's work of salvation:

"The Ascension of our Lord Jesus Christ. Our Lord went up Body and Soul into heaven in the sight of His apostles, by His own power, to take possession of His glory, and to be our Advocate and Mediator in heaven with the Father. He ascended as Man, as Head of the redeemed, and has prepared a dwelling in heaven for all those who follow in His steps."

What Do We Mean "Ascension"?

The physical, bodily ascension of Jesus is a foundational doctrine of the Christian faith. While the details of this event are not often emphasized from the pulpit, its significance carries profound implications for our hope as believers. To discuss the ascension meaningfully, it's important to first clarify what we mean by it.

To bring clarity, we must revisit the previous chapter. There, we established that a core belief of the Christian faith is the physical, bodily resurrection of Jesus. Scripture affirms that the tomb was empty and that Jesus was seen and recognized by His followers—not as a spiritual apparition or disembodied presence, but in a physical body. This body could be touched, it breathed, and it even ate. In short, Jesus was fully alive.

So what became of this resurrected and glorified body? Did Jesus eventually die again, with His spirit going to be with the Father? Absolutely not! When Jesus ascended, His resurrected body went with Him. This event took place 40 days after the resurrection and is recorded by Luke in *Acts*:

"After saying this, he was taken up into a cloud while they were watching, and they could no longer see him. As they strained to see him rising into heaven, two white-robed men suddenly stood among them. 'Men of Galilee,' they said, 'why are you standing here staring into heaven? Jesus has been taken from you into heaven, but someday he will return from heaven in the same way you saw him go!'"
Acts 1:9-11 NLT

While the language here uses spatial and geographical terms to describe Jesus' ascension, it is essential to focus on the significance of the event rather than just the narrative details. Jesus, being fully man and fully God, ascended both in body and spirit to the presence of God. This physical ascension underscores the truth of His humanity and divinity and assures us of His continuing role as our intercessor in heaven.

What Does the Old Testament Say About It?

The clearest Old Testament passage foretelling the ascension of Jesus is found in Psalm 68:18. This psalm, attributed to David, was likely sung when the ark was moved to Jerusalem. While it celebrates that historical event, like many of David's psalms, it also carries prophetic significance:

"When you ascended to the heights, you led a crowd of captives. You received gifts from the people, even from those who rebelled against you. Now the Lord God will live among us there."
Psalm 68:18 NLT

The Apostle Paul later references this passage in Ephesians 4:8-10, applying it directly to the ascension of Christ:

"That is why the Scriptures say, 'When he ascended to the heights, he led a crowd of captives and gave gifts to his people.' Notice that it says 'he ascended.' This clearly means that Christ also descended to our lowly world. And the same one who descended is the one who ascended higher than all the heavens, so that he might fill the entire universe with himself."
Ephesians 4:8-10 NLT

In addition to these direct references, shadows of the ascension can be traced back to the very beginning of creation. The Garden of Eden, which Ezekiel 28:13-14 describes as being on a mountain, serves as an early example of ascending into God's presence. Adam and Eve lived in this elevated "temple," where heaven and earth overlapped, and humanity communed directly with God. After the Fall, this pattern of ascending to God's presence continued, though now it involved sacrifices and mediators.

In Exodus, God commands Moses and the leaders of Israel to *"come up"* to Mount Sinai to meet with Him and receive instructions for the people. Moses ascends the mountain with the elders and enters the cloud of God's glory to commune with Him.

Another significant foreshadowing occurs in Leviticus, where the Day of Atonement (Yom Kippur) points to the need for atonement and reconciliation with God. On this holy day, the high priest would symbolically ascend into God's presence by passing through the veil in the tabernacle, moving from the human realm into God's holy space. This act, representing a yearly encounter with God, involved the sacrifice of animals to atone for the sins of the entire nation.

Throughout Scripture, this narrative of ascending into God's presence is a recurring theme. Adam and Eve, Moses, and the high priests all ascended to meet with God. Yet, after the Fall, these ascensions required sacrifices to bridge the gap between sinful humanity and a holy God. This culminates in Jesus, who is both the ultimate sacrifice and the Great High Priest. It is no surprise, then, that Jesus

Himself ascended into God's presence, fulfilling and surpassing all these earlier foreshadowings.

"For Christ did not enter into a holy place made with human hands, which was only a copy of the true one in heaven. He entered into heaven itself to appear now before God on our behalf."
Hebrews 9:24, NLT

Jesus' ascension represents the ultimate fulfillment of God's redemptive plan. As both the perfect sacrifice and our eternal High Priest, He ascended not into an earthly temple but into heaven itself, ensuring eternal access to God for all who believe in Him.

What Did Jesus Have to Say About It?

It's clear from Scripture that Jesus anticipated His return to the Father. While teaching at the Temple in Jerusalem, He made this statement:

"But Jesus told them, 'I will be with you only a little longer. Then I will return to the one who sent me. You will search for me but not find me. And you cannot go where I am going.'"
John 7:33-34 NLT

This was a warning from the Messiah that His earthly ministry was nearing its end. Notice, however, that Jesus not only knew this but clearly communicated His return to the Father. Even after His resurrection, Jesus understood and conveyed that there was more yet to come. In the Gospel of John, He spoke these words to Mary Magdalene:

"Don't cling to me," Jesus said, "for I haven't yet ascended to the Father. But go find my brothers and tell them, 'I am ascending to my Father and your Father, to my God and your God.'"
John 20:17 NLT

A Bible commentator reflected on this passage, stating:
"He also made specific mention of His coming ascension. The word of His ascension let them know He was raised never to die again."

In summary, Jesus was fully aware of His ascension, spoke about it with His followers, and looked forward to it with anticipation. His ascension signified the completion of His earthly mission and the beginning of His exalted reign at the right hand of the Father.

What Did the Early Church Believe?

From the very beginning, early Church leaders not only accepted the ascension of Jesus but taught its significance as an essential doctrine. One of the clearest references comes from the Apostle Peter in 1 Peter 3:22. Writing to *"God's chosen people who are living as foreigners in the provinces of Pontus, Galatia, Cappadocia, Asia, and Bithynia,"* Peter states:

"Now Christ has gone to heaven. He is seated in the place of honor next to God, and all the angels and authorities and powers accept his authority."
1 Peter 3:22 NLT

This is a direct reference to the ascension and Christ's exalted position at the right hand of God. The Apostle Paul also makes reference to the ascension, as we read earlier in Ephesians 4:8-10. Additionally, Paul highlights its importance in his letter to Timothy:

"Without question, this is the great mystery of our faith: Christ was revealed in a human body and vindicated by the Spirit. He was seen by angels and announced to the nations. He was believed in throughout the world and taken to heaven in glory."
1 Timothy 3:16 NLT

The writer of Hebrews also emphasizes the ascension as a crucial part of Jesus' work. Not only does it affirm that Jesus is in God's presence, but it also highlights His ongoing role as our High Priest, interceding on our behalf. This imagery draws parallels to the work of the high priest on the Day of Atonement, emphasizing Jesus' eternal priesthood and His role in fulfilling God's will for humanity:

"So then, since we have a great High Priest who has entered heaven, Jesus the Son of God, let us hold firmly to what we believe."
Hebrews 4:14, NLT

"This hope is a strong and trustworthy anchor for our souls. It leads us through the curtain into God's inner sanctuary. Jesus has already gone in there for us. He has become our eternal High Priest in the order of Melchizedek."
Hebrews 6:19-20 NLT

"So Christ has now become the High Priest over all the good things that have come. He has entered that greater, more perfect Tabernacle in heaven, which was not made by human hands and is not part of this created world."
Hebrews 9:11 NLT

Beyond the New Testament, the ascension is affirmed in early Church creeds, demonstrating its significance throughout Christian history. In the fourth century, the Athanasian Creed and the Apostles' Creed both confirmed this truth. Even earlier, in the second century, the Old Roman Creed (also known as the Old Roman Symbol) explicitly acknowledged the ascension. From the first letters circulated among believers to the early creeds of the Church, the ascension of Jesus was consistently taught as a foundational doctrine, underscoring its importance to Christian faith and theology.

Why Does It Matter?

God the Father sent the Son into the world at Bethlehem to carry out His divine will, and now, through the ascension, the Son was returning to the Father. The ascension marked the completion of Jesus' earthly mission and the beginning of His supreme authority over all creation. It signifies the success of His mission—His earthly work was finished, His purpose accomplished. Consider the ascension as a divine victory celebration. If there were more for Jesus to accomplish on Earth, He would have remained. His departure assures us that God's promises have been fulfilled and His mission completed.

The ascension also symbolizes the exaltation of Jesus by the Father. Paul describes this magnificently in his letter to the Ephesians, emphasizing Christ's supreme authority over all creation and His role as the head of the Church:

"Now he is far above any ruler or authority or power or leader or anything else—not only in this world but also in the world to come. God has put all things under the authority of Christ and has made him head over all things for the benefit of the church."
Ephesians 1:21-22, NLT

Jesus was received into glory with honor and was given the name above all names. Having perfectly carried out the Father's will, He was exalted to the highest place, as Paul writes in Philippians:

"Therefore, God elevated him to the place of highest honor and gave him the name above all other names."
Philippians 2:9, NLT

Furthermore, the ascension signifies the beginning of Jesus' ongoing role as our High Priest and Mediator of the New Covenant. In this role, He intercedes on our behalf before God the Father, continually advocating for us. The ascension assures us that Jesus is not only victorious but also actively working for our good even now.

What Does It Mean for Us?

Without the ascension of Christ, there would be no High Priest ruling and reigning over all creation, our assurance of heaven would be in serious doubt, and we would lack the indwelling Spirit of God to help us understand His truths. When considered in these terms, the ascension of Jesus is not merely an event in His life—it is essential to the life of every believer. Let's break this down and examine what we have as a result of a resurrected and ascended Savior.

First, the ascension gives us direct access to God's throne, where we can receive mercy and find grace in our time of need. Not only do we have access, but the writer of Hebrews assures us that we can approach God's throne boldly. This confidence is made possible because Jesus, our risen and ascended Savior, serves as our High Priest who fully understands our weaknesses:

"So let us come boldly to the throne of our gracious God. There we will receive his mercy, and we will find grace to help us when we need it most."
Hebrews 4:16 NLT

Second, the ascension made it possible for Jesus to send us the Advocate, the Holy Spirit. In John's Gospel, Jesus even declares that it is better for Him to go away so that the Holy Spirit could come:

"But in fact, it is best for you that I go away, because if I don't, the Advocate won't come. If I do go away, then I will send him to you."
John 16:7 NLT

While Jesus in His incarnate form was limited by space and time, the Holy Spirit is limitless. After the ascension, the Holy Spirit was sent to dwell within all believers, simultaneously empowering them with truth, guiding them in sanctification, growing spiritual fruit, and equipping them with gifts to carry out God's will. This Advocate works in and through us in ways that Jesus, in His earthly ministry, could not accomplish due to His physical limitations.

Additionally, Jesus ascended to "prepare a place" for us in heaven. This promise, recorded in the Gospel of John, gives believers confident hope in the eternal home that awaits us because of Jesus' finished work:

"There is more than enough room in my Father's home. If this were not so, would I have told you that I am going to prepare a place for you? When everything is ready, I will come and get you, so that you will always be with me where I am."
John 14:2-3 NLT

In summary, the ascension of Jesus Christ means we have a High Priest who rules and reigns over all creation, giving us bold access to God's throne of grace. It means the Holy Spirit dwells within us, transforming us into living temples through whom God works. Finally, it assures us of the eternal home Jesus is preparing for us, giving us hope and confidence in the promise of heaven. The ascension is not just a moment in history—it is a cornerstone of our faith and daily walk with God.

Further Study

1. What is the significance of Jesus' bodily ascension as described in passages like Acts 1:9-11 and Luke 24:50-53? How does it demonstrate His authority and glorification?

2. How does Jesus' ascension fulfill Old Testament prophecies and foreshadowing, such as Psalm 110:1 and Daniel 7:13-14?

3. What does Jesus' ascension reveal about His role as our High Priest and mediator at the right hand of God? (See Hebrews 4:14-16 and Romans 8:34.)

4. How does Jesus' promise to send the Holy Spirit (John 16:7) connect to His ascension, and why was this promise significant for the early Church and for believers today?

5. What does Jesus' bodily ascension teach us about His physical return? How is this emphasized in Acts 1:11 and other passages?

6. How does Jesus' ascension provide hope and encouragement for believers, both in their mission to spread the gospel and in their anticipation of eternal life with Him?

Additional Notes:

13. Jesus' Intercession

Key Terms

1. **Intercession** - Jesus' ongoing act of praying and advocating on behalf of believers before the Father, ensuring their salvation and access to God (Hebrews 7:25; Romans 8:34).
2. **Mediator** - Jesus' role as the sole bridge between God and humanity, reconciling them through His sacrifice and ongoing intercession (1 Timothy 2:5; Hebrews 9:15).
3. **Advocate** - A term describing Jesus as one who defends and supports believers, particularly when they sin, ensuring their standing before God (1 John 2:1; John 14:16).
4. **High Priest** - Jesus' role as the perfect High Priest who offered Himself as the ultimate sacrifice and continues to intercede for believers in God's presence (Hebrews 4:14-16; Hebrews 9:24).
5. **Atonement** - The work of Christ on the cross, which provides the basis for His intercession by reconciling sinners to God and satisfying divine justice (Romans 5:10; Colossians 1:20).
6. **Access** - The privilege believers have to approach God directly through Jesus' intercession, made possible by His sacrificial death and resurrection (Ephesians 2:18; Hebrews 10:19-22).

Christ has entered alone into the holy place, having Himself obtained eternal redemption for us. The solitary Surety on earth, He is the solitary Intercessor above. No other voice pleads with the Father; no other priest or minister, saint or angel, can be of any avail in coming between the sinner and God. - John Ross Macduff

What Do We Mean "Intercession"?

Before we examine the concept of intercession, let's briefly revisit the previous chapter where we discussed the bodily ascension of Jesus. After His resurrection, Jesus was taken up to heaven (Luke 24:51), where He ascended to a place of honor at the right hand of God (1 Peter 3:22). This ascension was not merely an act of glorification but also a step in fulfilling His role as our eternal High Priest (Hebrews 6:19-20). In doing so, Jesus brought the Levitical priesthood and sacrificial system to their ultimate fulfillment.

God had established the Levitical Priesthood and Sacrificial System through Moses. Under this system, priests were responsible for teaching and enforcing God's law. It was also through this system that individuals sought forgiveness for their sins through daily, weekly, and monthly sacrifices. One of the most significant aspects of this system was the Day of Atonement (Yom Kippur). On this solemn day, the High Priest would enter the Holy of Holies, the innermost chamber of the Temple, to intercede on behalf of the people, seeking forgiveness for the nation's sins and reconciling them to God through sacrifice.

However, this system was insufficient to fully address the problem of sin. It was temporary and could not permanently satisfy the just requirements of the Law. To accomplish this once and for all, Jesus became both the ultimate sacrifice and the eternal High Priest. As High Priest, He entered the true Holy of Holies in heaven—not a man-made replica—to intercede directly before God on our behalf. The writer of Hebrews explains this profound truth:

"For Christ did not enter into a holy place made with human hands, which was only a copy of the true one in heaven. He entered into heaven itself to appear now before God on our behalf."
Hebrews 9:24 NLT

This is the essence of Jesus' intercession. Intercession means intervening on behalf of another, and Jesus' intercession involves Him intervening on behalf of those who have placed their faith in Him. If you are united with Christ through faith, He is literally in the presence of the Father, pleading your case. Importantly, His advocacy is not based on your merit or works but entirely on who He is and the finished work He accomplished on the cross.

This incredible truth reminds us that our credibility before God is rooted in Jesus alone. His intercession offers us assurance that we are continually represented and justified before the Father, not by our righteousness but by His.

What Does the Old Testament Say About It?

First, I want to clarify that I am specifically addressing the intercession of Jesus on behalf of Christians. Intercession is a recurring theme throughout the Old Testament. For example, Abraham interceded for Lot and his family, and Moses interceded for the Hebrews in Egypt and in the wilderness. However, our focus here is on Jesus' role as our intercessor, a role that was foretold in Scripture. In Isaiah 53, we see a prophetic reference to the Messiah's work, including His role in intercession. Isaiah, under the inspiration of the Holy Spirit, predicted the coming Messiah hundreds of years before His arrival:

"I will give him the honors of a victorious soldier, because he exposed himself to death. He was counted among the rebels. He bore the sins of many and interceded for rebels."
Isaiah 53:12, NLT

This passage highlights that Jesus' bearing of our sins was only part of His redemptive mission. His work also includes ongoing intercession on behalf of rebels—those who have transgressed against God, as some translations state. This intercession reflects His compassionate role as mediator between God and humanity.

Beyond this direct reference in Isaiah, it's important to note that Jesus' role as intercessor fulfills the pattern established in the Law and the Levitical priesthood. The priests in the Old Testament acted as mediators, interceding for the people before God. Jesus, as the ultimate High Priest, not only fulfills but surpasses this role, offering Himself as the perfect sacrifice and continuing to intercede on behalf of His followers. I believe that Charles Spurgeon brings additional clarity with the following quote,

The greatest plea with God is Christ himself. The argument which always prevails with God is Christ incarnate, Christ fulfilling the law, and Christ bearing the penalty. Jesus himself is the reasoning and logic of prayer, and he himself is an ever living prayer unto the Most High. -Charles Spurgeon

What Did the Early Church Believe?

The doctrine of Jesus' intercession on our behalf was not only a belief held by the early Church but also a foundational teaching evident in their letters and practices. Paul, in his letter to the believers in Rome, makes this clear:

"Who then will condemn us? No one—for Christ Jesus died for us and was raised to life for us, and he is sitting in the place of honor at God's right hand, pleading for us."
Romans 8:34 NLT

Further evidence of this belief is found in the historical accounts of early Hebrew Christians who ceased participating in the Jewish sacrificial system. Even when faced with mounting pressure, criticism, and persecution, early Christians rejected the practice of seeking atonement through animal sacrifices. They understood that Jesus' death and resurrection had fulfilled the need for sacrifices once and for all. There was no longer a requirement for a priest to mediate between them and God, as Jesus had ascended to the position of eternal High Priest and now intercedes for them directly.

This truth was one of the key reasons the writer of Hebrews addressed his letter to Jewish believers, emphasizing the superiority of Christ's priesthood:

"Unlike those other high priests, he does not need to offer sacrifices every day. They did this for their own sins first and then for the sins of the people. But Jesus did this once for all when he offered himself as the sacrifice for the people's sins. The law appointed high priests who were limited by human weakness. But after the law was given, God appointed his Son with an oath, and his Son has been made the perfect High Priest forever."
Hebrews 7:27-28 NLT

Through His perfect sacrifice and ongoing intercession, Jesus has provided believers with direct access to God, eliminating the need for earthly mediators. This profound truth transformed the faith and practice of the early Church and continues to offer hope and assurance to believers today.

What Did Jesus Say About It?

One of my favorite passages concerning what Jesus said about His intercession is somewhat indirect but profoundly significant. It occurs near the end of His ministry, as Jesus explains to His disciples why His departure would actually benefit them. In the Gospel of John, Jesus reassures them, saying, *"I will ask,"* and because of His request, *"He will give"*—the *"He"* referring to God the Father. Isn't that amazing? Jesus is essentially saying, *"When I get to where I'm going, I'm going to intercede on your behalf and advocate for what you need."*

"And I will ask the Father, and he will give you another Advocate, who will never leave you."
John 14:16 NLT

Later, in John 17, we see Jesus praying before His betrayal. In this prayer, He intercedes for His disciples, asking for their protection, unity, sanctification, and more. This demonstrates Jesus stepping into His intercessory role even before His crucifixion.

"I am praying not only for these disciples but also for all who will ever believe in me through their message."
John 17:20 NLT

Perhaps one of the most powerful affirmations of Jesus' intercessory work comes from the Gospel of Matthew. Here, Jesus highlights the immense power of prayer when believers gather in His name. He promises that their prayers, offered in unity, will be heard and answered, underscoring His ongoing presence among them.

"I tell you the truth, whatever you forbid on earth will be forbidden in heaven, and whatever you permit on earth will be permitted in heaven. I also tell you this: If two of you agree here on earth concerning anything you ask, my Father in heaven will do it for you. For where two or three gather together as my followers, I am there among them."
Matthew 18:18-20 NLT

The Puritan theologian John Bunyan offers an insightful reflection in his work *"Christ—A Complete Saviour."* Although Bunyan's statement aligns closely with Hebrews 4:16, it resonates with the sentiment Jesus expresses in Matthew 18, emphasizing the powerful and personal intercession of Christ on behalf of His followers.

"Let this doctrine give thee boldness to come to God. Shall Jesus Christ be interceding in heaven? Oh, then, be thou a praying man on earth; yea, take courage to pray. Think thus with thyself — I go to God, to God, before whose throne the Lord Jesus is ready to hand my petitions

to him; yea, "he ever lives to make intercession for me." This is a great encouragement to come to God by prayers and supplications for ourselves, and by intercessions for our families, our neighbours, and enemies." - John Bunyan

Why Does It Matter?

When we rightly understand Jesus as our eternal High Priest, we can break down His role into distinct parts. The first is substitution—through His atoning sacrifice, Jesus bore our sins and made the payment on our behalf. The second is intercession—Jesus advocates for us and mediates before the Father on our behalf. In both roles, He acts as our guarantor. As Hebrews 7:22 states, *"Jesus guarantees this covenant between us and God."* This means we do not approach the Father based on our own word or deeds but solely on the merits of Christ's work.

Additionally, Jesus is uniquely qualified for this role because He is both fully God and fully man, perfectly embodying each nature. He alone understands our weaknesses and can honestly and effectively advocate for us. The author of Hebrews alludes to this in Hebrews 4:15:

"This High Priest of ours understands our weaknesses, for he faced all of the same testings we do, yet he did not sin."
Hebrews 4:15 NLT

Jesus was perfectly suited for the role of sacrifice, being the only One God would find acceptable. However, He is also perfectly suited as our intercessor. Having lived a full, though brief, human life, He understands our experiences and struggles firsthand, including facing temptations Himself. When Satan accuses us, Jesus' response—offered in His own blood—overrules every accusation, providing us with complete assurance of our standing before God.

Lastly, Jesus is not only the only human mediator between us and God—He is the only mediator, period. Despite what some traditions or teachings may claim, no one else—not Mary, not Christian saints, nor angels—has the power or authority to intercede for us before the throne of Almighty God. This unique role belongs to Christ alone. As Paul writes in 1 Timothy 2:5:

"For, There is one God and one Mediator who can reconcile God and humanity—the man Christ Jesus."
1 Timothy 2:5 NLT

Through His dual roles as our High Priest and Mediator, Jesus bridges the gap between humanity and God, ensuring our salvation, advocacy, and eternal relationship with the Father.

What Does It Mean For Us?

First and foremost, we should consider the unparalleled access we now have to God and the Holy Spirit because of Jesus' sacrifice and ongoing intercession. Jesus made it clear during His ministry that He would send the Holy Spirit to His followers, making them temples for the Spirit of God—not in a passive way, but actively working within them. Paul elaborates in Romans 8 on how the Holy Spirit helps us in our weakness, particularly by interceding on our behalf:

"And the Holy Spirit helps us in our weakness. For example, we don't know what God wants us to pray for. But the Holy Spirit prays for us with groanings that cannot be expressed in words."
Romans 8:26 NLT

This direct access to the living God is made possible through Christ! The significance of this access was symbolized at the moment of Jesus' death when "the veil" in the Temple was torn. This was no ordinary curtain but the one that separated the Holy of Holies—where God's presence dwelled—from the rest of the Temple. Only the High Priest could enter this sacred space, and only once a year. The tearing of the veil signified that, through Christ, all believers now have direct access to the Father.

"The light from the sun was gone. And suddenly, the curtain in the sanctuary of the Temple was torn down the middle."
Luke 23:45 NLT

And Jesus' work didn't end there. After His resurrection, Jesus spent weeks preparing His disciples for their mission, giving them the Great Commission before ascending into glory. Yet, His ascension didn't mark a period of rest. Jesus did not ascend to "take a break" until His second coming; rather, He remains actively involved, shepherding His people and interceding on their behalf in heaven. The writer of Hebrews highlights this ongoing role:

"There were many priests under the old system, for death prevented them from remaining in office. But because Jesus lives forever, his priesthood lasts forever. Therefore he is able, once and forever, to save those who come to God through him. He lives forever to intercede with God on their behalf."
Hebrews 7:23-25 NLT

The comparison between the Levitical priests and Jesus underscores the eternal nature of His priesthood. Unlike the priests of old, whose ministry ended with their death, Jesus' priesthood is eternal, enabling Him to save "once and forever." Some translations use the word "uttermost," derived from the Greek word *pantelés,* meaning complete, perfect, absolute, and enduring for all time. This salvation is not based on our efforts but on Christ, who *"lives forever to intercede with God on [our] behalf."* Paul reinforces this truth in Romans 8:

"Who then will condemn us? No one—for Christ Jesus died for us and was raised to life for us, and he is sitting in the place of honor at God's right hand, pleading for us."
Romans 8:34 NLT

Jesus completed His earthly work when He ascended to heaven, but His ministry continues through His intercession for us. John emphasizes this in a way that offers reassurance for those who stumble in their attempts to live fully for Christ:

"My dear children, I am writing this to you so that you will not sin. But if anyone does sin, we have an advocate who pleads our case before the Father. He is Jesus Christ, the one who is truly righteous."
1 John 2:1 NLT

Through Jesus' intercession, we experience grace upon grace. Our risen Savior is forever pleading our case and advocating for what we need to fulfill God's plan and purpose. Because of Him, we can approach the Father's throne with boldness, confident in the hope of salvation. Our ongoing acceptance before God is firmly grounded in the sufficiency of Christ's sacrifice on the cross, providing us with an unshakable foundation for our faith.

Further Study

1. What does the Bible teach about Jesus' role as our intercessor? Consider passages like Hebrews 7:25, Romans 8:34, and 1 John 2:1.
2. How does Jesus' intercession reflect His ongoing role as our High Priest, and how does this provide assurance for believers? (See Hebrews 4:14-16 and Hebrews 9:24.)
3. What is the significance of Jesus interceding "at the right hand of God"? How does this position highlight His authority and closeness to the Father?
4. How does Jesus' intercession demonstrate His love and commitment to believers, even after His death and resurrection?
5. What practical impact does Jesus' intercession have on a believer's prayer life, confidence in salvation, and relationship with God?
6. How can understanding Jesus' intercession encourage believers to approach God boldly in times of need, temptation, or failure?

Additional Notes:

14. The Second Coming of Jesus

Key Terms

1. **Second Coming** - The future event when Jesus Christ will return to earth in glory and power to fulfill God's ultimate plan for judgment, restoration, and His eternal reign (Matthew 24:30; Revelation 19:11-16).
2. **Parousia** - A Greek term meaning "arrival" or "coming," often used in the New Testament to refer to the second coming of Christ (1 Thessalonians 4:15; 2 Thessalonians 2:8).
3. **Judgment** - The act of Jesus at His return, where He will judge the living and the dead, rewarding the righteous and condemning the unrepentant (2 Corinthians 5:10; Revelation 20:11-15).
4. **Millennium** - The thousand-year reign of Christ mentioned in Revelation 20, interpreted differently by various theological traditions (premillennialism, amillennialism, postmillennialism) (Revelation 20:4-6).
5. **Rapture** - A term used to describe the event when believers will be caught up to meet Jesus in the air, often associated with His second coming (1 Thessalonians 4:16-17; 1 Corinthians 15:51-52).
6. **New Heaven and New Earth** - The renewed creation promised in Scripture, where believers will dwell with God eternally in perfect peace and righteousness after Jesus' return (Revelation 21:1-4; 2 Peter 3:13).

When considering the doctrine of the Second Coming, it's essential to remember that it stands at the very center of the Gospel message. The belief that Jesus will return is not contested among His Churches; it is a foundational truth of the Christian faith. However, this doctrine is accompanied by some interpretive challenges. The timing of His return, the events surrounding it, and how it will unfold have been topics of significant debate among believers. These discussions are often intertwined with related topics such as the Rapture and the seven years of Great Tribulation, which are closely connected to the Second Coming.

While these details may be debated, the most important truth to focus on is this: **Jesus is coming back!** This promise offers believers hope, assurance, and a reason to live with anticipation and readiness for His glorious return.

"The Second Coming of Jesus Christ is a cardinal doctrine of the Christian faith. It is not minor, it is not unimportant, it is not secondary or tertiary, it is critical. It is a substantial reality in our faith. In fact, in some ways the Second Coming of Jesus Christ is the most important of events because it's the end of the story, because the Second Coming consummates everything, everything. To minimize the Second Coming is to minimize everything else because this is the finale, the culmination. His return consummates the history of the world and the history of redemption and the fulfillment of all God's pledges and promises and covenants and threats and warnings. All blessing and all judgment in its final disposition is connected with the coming of Jesus Christ. World history seems sometimes to be a careening sort of helter-skelter, pell-mell into blackness, sort of uncontrolled. But that is not the case. While men's behavior becomes less and less controlled, the very movement of history is under the sovereign control of God, who is moving it inexorably, exactly to the point which He has predetermined, and that is the return of Jesus Christ." - John MacArthur

What Do We Mean By "Second Coming of Jesus"?

The second coming of Jesus is a central topic within the field of **Eschatology**, which is the doctrine of "last things." Eschatology addresses significant matters such as death, the afterlife, Heaven and Hell, the Second Coming of Jesus, the resurrection of the dead, the Rapture, the Tribulation, millennialism, the end of the world, the Last Judgment, and the New Heaven and New Earth. It's important to recognize that within the Christian faith, there are varying interpretations and opinions regarding these topics.

When we speak of the second coming of Jesus—also known as the Second Advent—we are not referring to another birth or merely a spiritual manifestation. Instead, we are speaking about the physical return of the incarnate Jesus, who will come in His full glory. This return will be personal, visible, and majestic. At His first coming, Jesus fulfilled many prophecies as a humble servant and the sacrificial Lamb of God. However, His second coming will be radically different. He will return as a mighty warrior and conquering King, leading the armies of Heaven to complete God's plan of ultimate justice and redemption.

There is significant debate among Christians regarding the timeline of eschatological events, particularly concerning the Rapture, the Tribulation, and the Second Coming. The Rapture, where Christ returns to gather His elect, is interpreted in three primary ways: pre-tribulation, mid-tribulation, and post-tribulation. These views differ in their interpretation of whether the Church will endure the Great Tribulation, be spared entirely, or experience only part of it. While these differing perspectives spark much debate, the universal agreement among Christians is that Jesus will return in the Second Coming.

This glorious event is both the foundation of Christian hope and an absolute certainty. Regardless of the specific timing or sequence of events, the promise of Jesus' return assures believers that God's plan will be fulfilled, bringing justice, restoration, and eternal peace.

What Does the Old Testament Say About It?

It may not be as widely recognized as one might assume, but the Second Coming of Christ is prophesied in the Old Testament scriptures. While much of the focus is typically placed on prophecies concerning the first Advent—especially in the context of the Christmas season—when examined more thoroughly, it becomes clear that Old Testament prophets spoke of two distinct Advents of the Messiah. Early interpretations often merged these events into a single arrival, leading many to expect the Messiah to come as a political or military leader who would overthrow Rome.

Many prophetic books in Scripture, including those by Micah, Isaiah, Daniel, and Zechariah, pointed toward the Messiah's coming. These books not only foretold His first Advent but also prophesied His death and resurrection. In addition, they provided glimpses of His ultimate return and final triumph. A key passage in Zechariah offers a powerful hint of His second coming:

"On that day the Lord will defend the people of Jerusalem; the weakest among them will be as mighty as King David! And the royal descendants will be like God, like the angel of the Lord who goes before them! For on that day I will begin to destroy all the nations that come against Jerusalem. "Then I will pour out a spirit of grace and prayer on the family of David and on the people of Jerusalem. They will look on me whom they have pierced and mourn for him as for an only son. They will grieve bitterly for him as for a firstborn son who has died."
Zechariah 12:8–10 NLT

In addition to this passage, the Old Testament contains many other prophecies that point to the ultimate triumph of Jesus and His future reign. These include passages in Zechariah (9:14–15; 12:10–14; 13:1), Amos (9:11–15), and Jeremiah (30:18; 32:44; 33:11, 26). These verses paint a picture of a victorious Messiah who will return to establish His kingdom, fulfilling God's promises and bringing restoration to His people.

What Did Jesus Say About It?

During His ministry, Jesus made several truths abundantly clear: He would die, He would be resurrected, He would return to the Father, and He would come again. These truths are central to our faith as Christians and are unanimously affirmed by the "true" Church. But what did Jesus specifically say about His return? Let's examine some of His statements, beginning in Matthew 24.

""So you, too, must keep watch! For you don't know what day your Lord is coming. Understand this: If a homeowner knew exactly when a burglar was coming, he would keep watch and not permit his house to be broken into. You also must be ready all the time, for the Son of Man will come when least expected."
Matthew 24:42-44 NLT

From this passage, we can take away three key points: first, Jesus is indeed coming back; second, no one knows the exact timing of His return; and third, we must always be ready. There is great comfort in the certainty of His return, but this also serves as a reminder to avoid falling into hysteria or being deceived by false teachers who claim to know "when." Instead, we are called to live every day with expectancy, keeping our lives aligned with God's will and remaining spiritually prepared.

Jesus further elaborates on His return in Matthew 25:

""But when the Son of Man comes in his glory, and all the angels with him, then he will sit upon his glorious throne. All the nations will be gathered in his presence, and he will separate the people as a shepherd separates the sheep from the goats. He will place the sheep at his right hand and the goats at his left."
Matthew 25:31-33 NLT

Here, Jesus affirms once again that His return will indeed take place. He also reveals that His return will bring judgment, where all nations will be gathered before Him. This final judgment will separate believers from unbelievers, just as a shepherd separates sheep from goats. It is a moment of accountability for all humanity, underscoring the importance of living in obedience to Him.

Finally, stepping out of Jesus' earthly ministry and into the Revelation of John, we see a vivid reminder of the imminence of His return:

"'Look, I am coming soon, bringing my reward with me to repay all people according to their deeds. I am the Alpha and the Omega, the First and the Last, the Beginning and the End."
Revelation 22:12-13 NLT

These words confirm not only the certainty of His return but also its purpose—to bring both reward and judgment. Jesus, as the Alpha and the Omega, encompasses all of history and eternity, ensuring that His return will fulfill God's ultimate plan for justice and redemption. For believers, this promise is both a call to faithful living and a source of enduring hope.

What Did the Early Church Believe?

Considering scriptural evidence, the words of Jesus, and the inspiration of the Holy Spirit, the early Church fathers understood from the very beginning that Jesus would return. Luke records an exchange between the disciples and "two white-robed men" in the opening chapter of Acts that affirms this truth:

"As they strained to see him rising into heaven, two white-robed men suddenly stood among them. "Men of Galilee," they said, "why are you standing here staring into heaven? Jesus has been taken from you into heaven, but someday he will return from heaven in the same way you saw him go!"
Acts 1:10-11 NLT

This declaration was not only shared with Luke but also taught and passed down by the disciples. Early Church fathers, such as

Hippolytus, echoed this belief. Hippolytus, who was likely born between 170-175 AD, identified himself as a disciple of Irenaeus, who in turn was a disciple of Polycarp—a direct disciple of John the Apostle. This connection to John, the writer of the Gospel and the Book of Revelation, lends credibility to Hippolytus' stance. He wrote:

"For as two advents of our Lord and Savior are indicated in the Scriptures, the one being His first advent in the flesh, which took place without honor by reason of His being set at naught, as Isaiah spoke of Him aforetime. " But His second advent is announced as glorious, when He shall come from heaven with the host of angels, and the glory of His Father, as the prophet saith, "Ye shall see the King in glory;" and, "I saw one like the Son of man coming with the clouds of heaven. And he came to the Ancient of days, and he was brought to Him. And there were given Him dominion, and honor, and glory, and the kingdom; all tribes and languages shall serve Him."

If Hippolytus truly learned from John's spiritual lineage, it is no surprise that he would hold firmly to the belief in Christ's return. John himself affirmed this doctrine in his epistle:

"And now, dear children, remain in fellowship with Christ so that when he returns, you will be full of courage and not shrink back from him in shame."
1 John 2:28, NLT

Other New Testament writers also emphasized this truth. Peter compared Christ's return to the sudden arrival of a thief and linked it to the final judgment:

"But the day of the Lord will come as unexpectedly as a thief. Then the heavens will pass away with a terrible noise, and the very elements themselves will disappear in fire, and the earth and everything on it will be found to deserve judgment."
2 Peter 3:10 NLT

The writer of Hebrews urged believers to live with an attitude of readiness, reminding them to encourage one another as they anticipated Christ's return:

"And let us not neglect our meeting together, as some people do, but encourage one another, especially now that the day of his return is drawing near."
Hebrews 10:25 NLT

Paul also affirmed the Second Coming in the opening chapter of his letter to the Philippians. He highlights how Christ's return will bring our sanctification to completion, underscoring our dependence on Jesus:

"And I am certain that God, who began the good work within you, will continue his work until it is finally finished on the day when Christ Jesus returns."
Philippians 1:6 NLT

The doctrine of the Second Coming is not an optional or peripheral belief. It has been central to God's plan from the beginning. The prophets recognized it, Jesus proclaimed it, and the Church has faithfully taught it from its inception. This hope remains a cornerstone of Christian faith, pointing us to the glorious return of Christ when all things will be made new.

Why Does It Matter?

Without Christ's return, there can be no final consummation of all things, including the restoration of creation. Peter, in his second letter, emphasizes that we should live holy and godly lives as we anticipate His return, even doing what we can to "hurry it along." His return will bring about the passing away of the old and the establishment of new heavens and a new earth, where righteousness will dwell. Peter describes this incredible transformation as follows:

"Since everything around us is going to be destroyed like this, what holy and godly lives you should live, looking forward to the day of God and hurrying it along. On that day, he will set the heavens on fire, and the elements will melt away in the flames. But we are looking forward to the new heavens and new earth he has promised, a world filled with God's righteousness."
2 Peter 3:11-13 NLT

Without Christ's return, there is also no eternal reward for the redeemed or eternal punishment for the wicked. His return signifies the final judgment, where the destinies of all humanity will be revealed. In Matthew 25, Jesus vividly describes the separation of the righteous and the wicked, highlighting the eternal consequences of each group's actions and decisions:

"Then the King will say to those on his right, 'Come, you who are blessed by my Father, inherit the Kingdom prepared for you from the creation of the world.'"
Matthew 25:34 NLT

"Then the King will turn to those on the left and say, 'Away with you, you cursed ones, into the eternal fire prepared for the devil and his demons.'"
Matthew 25:41 NLT

Christ's return is central to God's ultimate plan for creation, justice, and redemption. It will usher in a new reality where the faithful are rewarded with eternal life in His presence, and evil is permanently defeated. As believers, we are called to live in eager expectation of that day, grounded in the hope and assurance of His promises.

What Does It Mean For Us?

The Second Coming of Jesus is the ultimate hope for believers everywhere. It points to His sovereignty, reminds us of His faithfulness, and confirms the truth of His Word and the fulfillment of prophecy. It assures us of His victory over sin and death and gives us confidence in the salvation of our mortal bodies. Through His return, we are promised glorified, resurrected bodies—pure, immortal, and incorruptible. Paul addresses this hope in his second letter to the Corinthians:

"For we know that when this earthly tent we live in is taken down (that is, when we die and leave this earthly body), we will have a house in heaven, an eternal body made for us by God himself and not by human hands."
2 Corinthians 5:1 NLT

Beyond the promise of a transformed body, Jesus assures us with His own words that His return will usher us into our eternal home—a heavenly dwelling where we will live with Him forever:

"Don't let your hearts be troubled. Trust in God, and trust also in me. There is more than enough room in my Father's home. If this were not so, would I have told you that I am going to prepare a place for you? When everything is ready, I will come and get you, so that you will always be with me where I am."
John 14:1-3 NLT

Paul also spoke to the Thessalonians about this hope, describing the Second Coming and the rapture of believers. He encouraged them to hold on to this promise as a source of comfort and strength, reminding them to "encourage each other with these words." This hope of being united with Christ offers deep reassurance to believers:

"We tell you this directly from the Lord: We who are still living when the Lord returns will not meet him ahead of those who have died. For the Lord himself will come down from heaven with a commanding shout, with the voice of the archangel, and with the trumpet call of God. First, the believers who have died will rise from their graves. Then, together with them, we who are still alive and remain on the earth will be caught up in the clouds to meet the Lord in the air. Then we will be

with the Lord forever. So encourage each other with these words."
1 Thessalonians 4:15-18 NLT

The Second Coming of Christ will not only fulfill His promises but also establish His reign and bring to completion everything believers have hoped and longed for. It is the culmination of God's redemptive plan, a moment of ultimate triumph when Jesus will reign as King, and we will dwell with Him eternally.

Further Study

1. What does the Bible teach about the second coming of Jesus? Consider key passages such as Matthew 24:30-31, Acts 1:10-11, and Revelation 19:11-16.
2. How does Jesus' promise of His return provide hope and encouragement for believers, as described in John 14:1-3 and 1 Thessalonians 4:16-18?
3. What are some of the signs and events the Bible says will precede Jesus' second coming? How should believers interpret these signs? (See Matthew 24:4-14 and 2 Thessalonians 2:1-4.)
4. How does the second coming of Jesus demonstrate God's justice, authority, and ultimate victory over evil? (See 2 Thessalonians 1:7-10 and Revelation 20:11-15.)
5. What is the difference between the second coming of Jesus and the rapture? How do various interpretations of these events shape Christian eschatology?
6. How should the promise of Jesus' return influence the way believers live their daily lives, as instructed in 2 Peter 3:11-14 and Titus 2:11-14?

Additional Notes:

Made in the USA
Coppell, TX
02 February 2025

45321496R00098